# The
# Complete
# Golf Course

# The Complete Golf Course

---

## turf and design

---

by

Claude Crockford

Published 1993 by
Thomson Wolveridge & Associates Pty Ltd
11 Crawford Street, Mt Eliza,
Victoria 3930, Australia

ISBN 0 646 13031 5

Limited to 1000 copies

This copy numbered....................*734*...........................

...............................................................................................................

Photography by Roger Gould, Harley Kruse, Peter Thomson
Typeset by Abb-typesetting Pty Ltd, Collingwood, Victoria
Designed by Peter Yates
Printed by South China Printing Co., Hong Kong

# Contents

# Foreword

Claude Crockford was course manager for the Royal Melbourne Golf Club for some 40 years and I was fortunate enough to be associated with him for nearly 20 years of that time.

As chairman of the Green Committee for some eight years, I was in the position of being able properly to appreciate his unrivalled skill in maintaining the character and condition of the two courses during a period when many international tournaments were staged at the Club, and it would be true to say that his reputation extended far beyond Australia.

This book contains information collected over these years, which should be of tremendous help to all who are connected, directly or indirectly, with the care of sports turf, whether it be on a golf course, sports arena or at home. The information comes in a form readily accessible to all.

It was this ability to convey information that made him so good at bringing the entire grounds staff to a peak of efficiency maintained over many years and through many difficult periods.

It is with great pleasure that I commend this book, not only as fascinating reading, but as a text book to be treasured by all lovers of fine turf.

G.P.H. BURGESS
Captain (1964–9) and President (1970–5)
Royal Melbourne Golf Club
20 June 1981

# Preface

No one passing by comes away with any other view than that Royal Melbourne is an exceptional place to play golf. What catches the eye is its spaciousness and the classic architecture of its designer Dr Alister Mackenzie. Each of its 36 holes is a gem. Most have awesome bunkers and large undulating greens like no other. These features help to make Royal Melbourne famous.

Yet as striking as these aspects are, they are not what lingers on in the mind long after. It is rather the texture and speed of the greens that we remember, because until recently, Royal Melbourne greens were uniquely the truest and fastest on earth. And they were so because of the skill and art of one man — Claude Crockford — who nurtured and maintained them for 40 years, until he retired in 1975.

Crockford joined the maintenance staff of Royal Melbourne Golf Club as a young man craving a career 'out of doors', soon after the construction began. In a few years he became the Head Greenkeeper — the Golf Course Superintendent. In the long years of an astonishing career, he developed a special program of preventative control and care that supported his grasses and plants in their own struggles with predators. His success was astonishing. In those 40 years through flood, frosts and devastating droughts, those greens were never less than perfect. The fairways may have suffered stresses and strains. His greens never. Nor did he ignore the dynamics of the rest of the landscape of Royal Melbourne. He knew every small plant and variety hidden in the indigenous 'bush' setting — even their botanical Latin names. He played no small part in their preservation.

One is tempted to use the title 'Genius' for Claude Crockford but he would be the last one to assume such a mantle. This book is his manual of care and attention — his life's work and a magnificent achievement by a most uncommon man.

In his modesty he explains his love affair with nature. If nature could communicate, it might acknowledge a reciprocation, for its response to his administrations over all those years indicated a most sympathetic understanding.

At a time when the high cost of energy, water and labour taunt today's golf courses to suffer huge annual maintenance expense; when the trend to return to a less complex and costly approach to golf course turf management gathers increasing necessity worldwide, Claude Crockford's superb work may afford the modern Golf Course Superintendent a practical alternative for consideration.

The Royal Melbourne turf will be his Shrine of Remembrance — a tribute to an uncommon genius.

PETER W. THOMSON CBE
Melbourne 1993

# Preface

Claude Crockford is like a gold nugget — rare and precious. He retired as custodian of Royal Melbourne Golf Club's courses with the reputation of Australia's foremost golf course superintendent — the doyen of them all.

How appropriate, then, that between the covers of this book — a collector's item immediately it was published — he should reveal the secrets of his wonderfully creative years at Royal Melbourne. More than anybody he made 'tick' Royal Melbourne's superb broad acres and brought them to a pitch that prompted Peter Thomson to say the course should be enshrined as a 'national treasure'.

Claude Crockford's first ambition was to become an architect but after several years of intense study at Swinburne College, the Depression and pressing family needs forced him to abandon the course and seek work.

He joined the staff of Yarra Bend public golf course and received his grounding there before being offered a position at Royal Melbourne to assist the club's ailing head greenkeeper, Mick Morcom. When failing health forced Morcom's retirement Claude Crockford was appointed to replace him and for over 40 years, until his own retirement in 1975, was in charge of caring for the most famous golf country in Australia.

He well remembers the days when the club's heavy equipment was horse-drawn and he used to tour the course in a jinker pulled by the club's pony, 'Creamy'.

Crockford's fine tuning of the courses he inherited from the great Dr Alister Mackenzie and Alec Russell cemented Royal Melbourne's position as Australia's number one golf test and lifted it into the top ten of the world's great golf courses. Throughout Australia, but more precisely his home state of Victoria, he set examples and created precedents that brought others to his doorstep, thirsty for the knowledge that he would so generously pass on.

Posterity will be the beneficiary of Claude Crockford's vast reservoir of knowledge, most of it contained in this excellent publication. His disciples are spread far and wide, all attempting to emulate the standards he set during his time at Royal Melbourne, a period in which he effectively rewrote the manual on golf course care and maintenance.

He brought to his occupation a professionalism that demands the recognition this publication gives him.

DON LAWRENCE
Melbourne 1993

# Acknowledgements

My thanks are due to the council of the Royal Melbourne Golf Club for giving permission to describe and photograph attractive and instructive features throughout the courses for inclusion in this book.

I thank Mr George Burgess, a prominent member of Royal Melbourne, for his interest and for so generously giving his time to editing the manuscript, and supplying a number of photographs.

During my long stay at Royal Melbourne I was often agreeably surprised by the willingness of the club members to help in the preparation of the course whenever the club was called on to stage a major tournament. My staff and I greatly appreciated the number of volunteers who came forward to assist in a type of work to which many of them were unaccustomed.

Two days before the event was due to start the volunteers would come to the club's workshop area to collect all the freshly painted equipment needed to ensure the proper control and running of an important golf tournament — items such as gallery control ropes and stakes. I would advise them to wear gardening gloves for the job, which was heavy and dirty and often carried out in hot weather. It could quickly raise blisters on hands not used to this type of labour.

The club members proved highly efficient and worked speedily at their appointed tasks and I was always very grateful for their assistance.

I also received assistance from another direction on many occasions in the form of comments from Peter Thomson and Michael Wolveridge, who always expressed their interest in what I was doing at Royal Melbourne. Their admiration for Royal Melbourne and its condition delighted me and was one of many factors which made me feel my years spent at the club had been well worthwhile.

CLAUDE CROCKFORD
Mount Eliza 1993

Part one

# Design and construction of golf course features

Golf course design should resemble as far as possible the pleasing profiles and contours of so many gentler small-scale natural formations.

Prior to the visit to Victoria in 1926 of Dr Alister Mackenzie, the acknowledged doyen of golf course architecture, this science did not exist in Australia as it is understood today. In those earlier times it was customary for planners to interpret formation of greens, tees, bunkers and mounds on right angle plans with flat green surfaces at the end of parallel-sided fairways.

All evidence of this severe and unnatural style that existed at Royal Melbourne — and elsewhere — has long since been removed or altered to become part of the present design, with the exception of several examples of old mounds that still exist and continue to influence play on the West course. These take the form of rough triangular prisms constructed across the line of play, and are now primarily of historical interest.

In the course of the transformation it soon became obvious that the sweeping curves defining large deeply carved hazards, irregular outlined and terraced tees with gently sloping sides, and fairways bounded by a series of long crescent shapes, often to a dog-leg plan, with undulating and beautifully moulded greens skilfully sited, were some of the essentials in the Mackenzie style of golf course architecture. These were to continue to prove testing and interesting to all who would play the course.

The terrain at Royal Melbourne with its easy rises and falls combined with high porosity soil, which may easily be moulded to any number of design variations, are attributes particularly appreciated by golf course architects.

In planning the West course all the natural features were totally exploited, so that upon a close study of the course today, it is difficult to imagine how a change at any

At Royal Melbourne, pre-1925 mounds still in existence at the 14th West Course. These features could more correctly be called hummocks as opposed to the flowing proportions of the mound construction that is so important in golf course design today.

Two examples of earlier mound work, circa 1910, which still influence play at several holes on the West Course at Royal Melbourne.

The 16th West Course at Royal Melbourne, 195 m – par 3. The treasured rough extends from tee to fairway, and contains a fine collection of dwarf indigenous plants, which are delightful in spring time.
Examples of more subtle old mound work can be seen in the middle-ground.
Design features include expansive bunkering, leaving a narrow area of turf to approach the green. Other bunkers on the right of the green, and not seen in the picture, are visible from an elevated tee.
Note that the bunkers on the left are raised considerably, with the remainder graduating to the fairway turf in the front.

hole would produce anything better, and any such suggestion would be difficult to justify.

Add to this the placement and design of the extensive bunkering denoting the more direct carry to a green, with the way around always provided for the shorter shot, essential for golf for pleasure as well as contributing towards an exacting championship test.

Such ideal ground formation is no longer available for golf course construction as it was fifty years ago, so land often with less favourable characteristics must be accepted to cater for the ever increasing number of golfers throughout the country.

Many fine courses have been, and are still being built on what was formerly flat uninteresting terrain; it is now possible with the use of modern earth-moving machinery to effectively and economically construct distinctive mounds and undulations which, if complemented with trees, can result in a natural looking layout with such interest and variety that it is difficult to reconcile with the original formation.

In most instances imitation of features at Royal Melbourne is difficult to achieve; nevertheless the many characteristics, both natural and artificial, provide an ideal example for study and discussion by students of golf course architecture and design, and an understanding of why it is so difficult to distinguish these two forms one from the other on these courses.

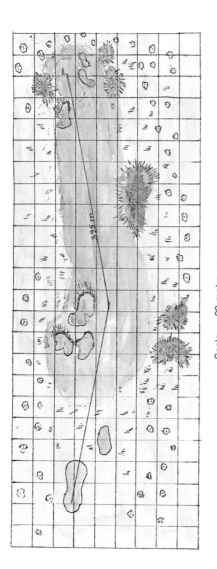

Scale — 20 metre squares
395 metres par 4

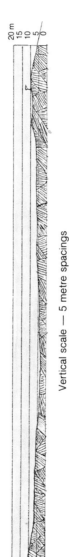

Vertical scale — 5 metre spacings
section on line to green
395 m

A concept for a par 4 hole.

# 1

# Mounds and hollows

Mounds should always be formed with attractive proportions and flowing profiles when viewed from any direction, gently grading from the higher land and fading out with finesse at the lower levels. When these recommendations are adhered to, the mounds can be economically mowed to perfection, which is always important.

Alternatively, anything that in any way resembles a dumped dollop of soil in this context should be avoided.

The vision and expertise required to merge new work into the natural formation are equally relevant when a flat featureless area has to be altered significantly to produce a discernible character, an effect produced largely with variations of mounds and hollows.

In this context the skill of an architect can be fully appreciated if, following large-scale earthworks and studied tree planting, pleasant vistas open up from the tees with each fairway adequately defined.

The scope of a plan should enable any original characteristic that may be modified or extended to be taken into consideration and possibly become a significant mark in a new layout. This is clearly demonstrated at Royal Melbourne by the manner in which the greens are nestling into the end of the fairways, and one can imagine the artistry and skill required with mound and hollow formation to create a concept in which there is so little difference between that produced by humans and the natural features.

All mound formation, irrespective of height, should have a similarity of profile wherever placed.

The base area of any mound is governed by the height desired by the architect at that particular point. An approximate guide for the construction of mounds and hollows of correct proportions, and therefore a natural appearance, is to maintain a maximum height of one tenth the diameter of the base.

Plans may vary from a simple circular outline, to an irregular design which ensures variations in heights.

Similar principles are involved when constructing hollows as depths and widths must be determined together, and follow a design which will impart a natural appearance to the work, and also allow efficient mowing.

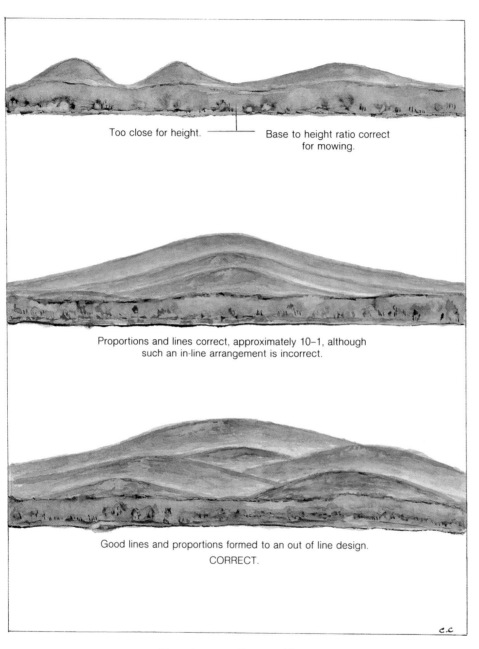

Too close for height. ———|——— Base to height ratio correct
for mowing.

Proportions and lines correct, approximately 10–1, although
such an in-line arrangement is incorrect.

Good lines and proportions formed to an out of line design.
CORRECT.

Mounds: proportions and lines.

Groups of mounds and hollows are often constructed on an extensive scale on fairways and approaches to greens as strategic features; they also enable bunkers to be formed and clearly defined within their structure.

A perfect example of delicate moulding may be seen in the formation of the mound at the back of the 1st green West course Royal Melbourne. It is low and spreading over a large area, with spines that are difficult to detect extending and diminishing well into the surface of the green and surrounding turf. Originally, and because it occupies such a large area, it could have been cast higher and remained well-proportioned. Had this been done, however, the subtlety of the gently tapered slopes would have been lost.

There are many examples of striking mound and hollow design throughout both courses at Royal Melbourne. A particular case involves the area surrounding the 18th green East course, where beautifully designed undulations are apparent from whatever angle they are viewed, although they cover a more extensive area to the right of the green.

A number of purposefully contrived hollows elsewhere are especially noteworthy; for instance, those that extend from the greens in a slightly diagonal direction and have a bearing on many approach shots are therefore distinctive. This type of feature is well illustrated at the 2nd, 3rd, and 17th West course; it is noticeable in each case how the lowest arc, or the bottom of the hollow, follows a curved line throughout its length, a revelant detail of hollow design.

An important element in planning a group of mounds is that they never appear to form lines, or seem crowded. Therefore sufficient space is essential for the correct proportions to be maintained. It is also important that those in the foreground be lower than those forming the background.

Attractive undulations, subtly moulded as an extension of the 3rd West Course green at Royal Melbourne, and which may be mown correctly with the fairway machine.

Soil type plays a significant role in the formation of mounds and hollows and the methods of their construction.

Where there is an obvious tendency to retain water, provision must be made as the work proceeds to ensure that drainage is adequate in any feature that is designed to influence play.

However, where the soil is of a sandy porous nature, as is the case at Royal Melbourne and other courses in the area, drainage difficulties are minimal, allowing an architect greater creativity when designing mound and hollow features on the course than with similar work on heavier type soil. In such cases it is often more practical to import suitable soil to form the features of the design. On the other hand, with land that has a depth of workable soil forming an undulating terrain, it is important for any additional construction required by the design to follow the natural character of the area rather than appear conspicuous or obtrusive when completed.

In planning a modern course it is advisable to consider the inclusion of viewing points, particularly if the course may in the future be the venue for important tournaments that will attract many visitors. These may be in the form of large mounds situated at points where it would be possible to watch tee and approach shots, as well as putting on one or two greens.

---

*Although the formation of mounds and hollows is contrary in principle, they must have a natural appearance that may be mown exactly, particularly where one feature flows to the other.*

---

# 2

# Trees and shrubs as part of course design

Golf courses generally are considered to be ideal places for extensive tree planting. Any such project, however, must be carefully planned, with an understanding of the turf problems trees can cause as and when they mature. Therefore it is extremely important to study the form and growth habits of any trees you may consider selecting for plantations bordering turf.

Once large trees are established in a prominent position too close to turf, their aesthetic value usually takes precedence over their removal, despite the fact that they often cause much unproductive maintenance work.

When tees are sited as far back as possible to obtain distance, and this occurs close to a boundary fence, it is not uncommon for trees to be planted to form a necessary screen without considering the type of trees most suitable for this situation. As their main purpose in this instance is to provide privacy, they need be a reasonable height only, with dense foliage from the ground up. This still allows sufficient sunshine to reach the turf for healthy growth. Any species planted on a boundary should be sited to avoid damage to fencing as they mature.

Tall dense plantations restrict air currents, with consequent high summer temperatures, and humidity which is conducive to turf grass problems. The roots also encroach as the trees mature.

Trees are often planted in strategic positions to influence play on a hole; in this situation, large trees with corresponding root systems are necessary with the inevitable development of weakness in the adjacent fairway turf.

Many of the finest strategic golf courses are in Scotland, and are practically treeless owing to their situation close to the coast, where strong prevailing winds that carry salt spray create an inhospitable environment. In addition, the severe unsheltered sand-dune terrain covered with a profusion of hardy dwarf plants contributes to an unsurpassed rugged naturalness and inimitable playing conditions.

With just a few exceptions, such conditions do not exist on Australian golf courses where tree culture provides a successful alternative. However, there are many examples of overcrowded planting, specifically where the rough is narrowed between fairways, and also near greens. This indicates that tree planting has had

10

precedence over fundamental turf maintenance, a situation which could have been forestalled by more careful planning.

Although Australian native trees have all the necessary attributes for golf course planting, an occasional exotic specimen, either evergreen or deciduous and chosen for a particular location on the course, can provide a distinctive contrast in the planting arrangements.

Planning of plantations must take into account varieties of different shapes to avoid creating any effect of an avenue: straight line planting is undesirable on golf courses, except in restricted areas. Generally, tree spacings should provide for full development without crowding at maturity.

A significant and economical aspect of tree planting in this highly mechanised age is the importance of providing facility for mowing between trees in the playing area wherever practical.

Any tree lost through fire, wind storm, drought or maybe insect or disease activity, should be replaced as soon as possible. It is an advantage to begin with a landscape plan showing locations and names of species, which can be referred to at times of failure.

Correct procedures for the planting and care of young trees can often mean the difference between optimum growth and sluggish progress. It is therefore important for the hole to be well prepared as this is where successful growth of any tree really begins. Up to this point it has usually been nurtured in a more sheltered position.

Hole sites should be cleared of all vegetation over twice the diameter of the hole, which is usually about 60cm. The top spade depth is first put aside while the second depth of soil is turned and broken up in the hole, the top soil then being returned in a clean well broken-up state. Any soil considered unsuitable should be replaced.

Most young plants benefit from the addition of a little cow manure, or blood and bone plus potash, deeply and thoroughly mixed into the soil.

When tree sites in heavy soils indicate water-holding problems, they should be built up above the natural surface with good soil and/or drainage pipes laid to relieve the situation. More suitable species should be selected for such conditions.

The optimum time for tree planting in Victoria is late autumn or early winter when the soil is thoroughly and deeply moist; deciduous species are best planted in the winter to early spring.

Careful staking, tying, watering and mulching are essential as each tree is planted; the final formation of the soil, under normal conditions should retain the water around the tree rather than allow it to flow away.

Some form of initial protection is usually desirable, particularly when the young plants are sited in cold or exposed positions. A shield of hessian or brush on the weather side would provide necessary shelter.

The species *Eucalyptus botryoides* — mahogany gum — is a majestic tree of some 18 metres in height, but should not be grown within 18 metres of mown turf. Many instances have occurred on golf courses where this tree and species of pines — mostly *Pinus radiata* — which are often self-sown, have been allowed to mature too close to turf. Both have expansive roots, many close to the surface, and are also troublesome because of their habit of continuously shedding leaves and twigs. *Eucalyptus viminalis* — manna gum — is another common species which will cause similar problems.

There are a number of eucalypts that are suitable for golf course planting, but

*Leptospermum laevigatum* (Coastal Tea-tree) displays masses of white blossom in October.

must always be sited with turf maintenance in mind. They may include *E. citriodora*, *E. ficifolia*, *E. forrestiana*, *E. leucoxylon*, *E. maculata*, and *E. calophylla*.

There is also a wide variety of other native species which are attractive in every way. They are greatly appreciated by the bird life, and should be selected especially for this reason. Such a group could embrace species of *Acacia, Agonis, Banksia, Callistemon, Grevillea, Kunzea, Leptospermum, Melaleuca* and *Thryptomene*. There are varieties within these species of widely diverse heights and shapes, so it is possible to follow specified plantings.

Suggested foreground planting near greens and tees may consist of smaller varieties of acacia and grevillea with thryptomene grading to broader and taller trees in the background. Consideration to shading of the turf, and spacing of the specimens to permit air circulation at maturity, are both important for the health of the turf.

There are several other suitable native species worthy of consideration for golf course planting, for example, *Callitris collumellaris* — Murray pine — is a hardy conifer, freely adaptable, with fine compact foliage, and tall erect form, a distinct contrast to other Australian native trees.

Angophoras are closely related to, and resemble, the eucalypts, are hardy and shapely, with creamy white flowers in the late spring; *Angophora cordifolia*, if given sufficient space, may be relied upon to develop into attractive trees.

*Leptospermum laevigatum* — tea tree — also known as the coast tea tree, is often grown successfully inland. Similar to the two species mentioned above, they are very hardy, require little maintenance, and damage from pests is negligible. They have masses of small white flowers in the springtime and when grown *en masse* they are seen at their best at this time of year.

Once a tea tree plantation has been well established self-sown plants are common and may be transplanted elsewhere; also further germinations can be encouraged by burning several branches, cut from mature trees, in a small clearing which can be left undisturbed until the young plants are ready to be transplanted when about 30cm high.

Two years after being transplanted, several light prunings to encourage the plants to grow upwards and out from the lower trunk are beneficial, thus forming the basis for the development of strong erect plants. On the other hand, when allowed to grow naturally they tend to lean against each other for support in plantations, eventually falling to an acute angle, often growing into grotesque forms that are eye-catching and charming but which in certain situations often leads to difficulties with course maintenance.

This species of tea tree may also be planted as a hedge, becoming quite dense with regular trimming.

On a number of golf courses, mostly those situated on sandy soils, there is a variety of dwarf native plants which, if in sufficient numbers, can provide the ideal rough for golf. All these plants are extremely hardy and slow growing with exquisitely coloured flowers in the spring. Unfortunately, however, they cannot compete with perennial grasses and also succumb to too frequent mowing.

In earlier days such plants were recorded growing profusely over a wide area around Port Phillip Bay with other scattered communities as far afield as Malvern. Today fragmented colonies only remain with a greatly reduced number of species. Examples can be seen in much of the rough of the courses of the Royal Melbourne Golf Club where many varieties continue to thrive because they have been allowed to grow undisturbed over many years.

If colonies of such plants are part of the environment of a site for a golf course, they should be considered as a valuable asset in the planning process.

The rugged beauty of some hardy old Tea-trees, posed at various angles, and unaffected by their exposed position.

Royal Melbourne West Course, showing hardy native grasses growing over a section of sandy rough near the 10th green.

*Ricinicarpos pinifolius* (Wedding Bush) among native shrubs and dwarf plants.

Springtime! Examples of indigenous vegetation retained as an integral part of bunker complexes for erosion control and natural beauty.

Whenever they are growing within sections that will require mowing, this operation should be kept to a minimum and not lower than 10cm, and after flowering if possible. Fertilisers or lime must not be applied to these plants, and care exercised to avoid any contact with herbicides.

These considerations for their well-being tends to indicate fragility. This is far from being the case, as frequently they will germinate and reproduce under natural conditions in sub-surface sand, and after the top soil has been removed, which often denotes extremely arid conditions. However, all stronger plants such as acacias, tea trees, etc. that germinate must be removed from the vicinity of the dwarf plants.

Despite the fact that they are low-growing, many of these plants are endowed with a strong deep woody root system; the roots often develop quickly being much deeper than the height above the ground may suggest, thus making transplanting difficult; a typical example is *Ricinicarpos pinifolius* — wedding bush — which usually defies all efforts at transplantation. However, there are a number of shallow-rooted species which may be successfully moved if lifted with a ball of soil during the winter, and replanted *en masse* to form a characteristic collection.

This form of planting is sometimes used with good effect to prevent wind erosion in large areas of bunker sand, adding an attractive feature to the hazard at the same time. In constructing such a feature, it is necessary to form an island to an irregular outline raised above the bunker floor, and with a convex surface, in which a variety of the native plants are closely planted and watered.

Noted below is a selection of hardy dwarf native plants suitable for planting in the situations described:

| | |
|---|---|
| *Aotus ericoides* | — aotus |
| *Chorizema cordatum* | — chorizema |
| *Correa reflexa* | — native fuchsia |
| *Dillwynia ericifolia* | — heathy parrot pea, or egg and bacon |
| *Eutasia microphylla* | — eutasia |
| *Gahnia radula* | — sword grass |
| *Patersonia fragilis* | — short purple flag |
| *Patersonia glabrata* | — wild iris, or leafy purple flag |
| *Stackhousia spathulata* | — coast stackhousia |
| *Stylidium graminifolium* | — trigger plant |
| *Themeda australis* | — kangaroo grass |
| *Wahlenbergia gracilis* | — austral bluebell |

*A balance in the layout is essential to provide interest as well as a test of skill.*

*Upon maturity of the work, the difficulty should then be to detect the natural from the man-made formations.*

Examples of dwarf native plants carefully retained in rough areas of the course.

# 3

## The tees

The teeing ground, as defined by the rules of golf, is a rectangular area formed by two markers which define the forward and side limits, the depth being calculated as two club lengths from the markers.

While it is essential that the actual teeing surfaces be flat and firm, the design should be such that the surface merges into the contours of the surrounding turf.

The first hole, West Course; 392 m – par 4. The tee is expansive and on the same level as the surrounding turf. The drive area is broad and without hazards, which allows players to move toward the green without much difficulty — a perfect first hole.

Royal Melbourne West Course, 6th hole, 391 m and the 10th hole, 279 m. Both present examples of terraced tee formations.

Often, however, the outline of the tee is defined by straight lines to a rectangular shape, where some character could be obtained simply by mowing the flat surface to an irregular outline.

There are a number of attractive examples of tee formation at Royal Melbourne at particular holes where groups of tees are terraced from the higher to the lower levels with turfed slopes between, all being mown into one continuous sward.

Although terrain must to a large extent determine formation, it is always important to strive for that often elusive natural effect. This can be enhanced in the initial stages by starting the level surface from a point which will avoid any impression of its having been built up as a whole, but rather that the tee is there as part of the surrounding space.

Occasionally, however, it becomes necessary to raise the tee so that players can see the drive area of a fairway, or the surface of a green, or because the situation is subject to occasional flooding.

Where a steep slope is involved with a tee site, obviously another steep slope on the lower side of the site will result; in this situation it is important that such grades be extended during the initial construction to facilitate tractor mowing.

The old style of raised rectangular tees lined up exactly to the fairway has little significance in modern golf course construction. The line for the tee shot is customarily accepted as being at right angles to the line set by the two markers, which are carefully placed to indicate this principle. The ladies' tees, although some distance forward, should conform to the same recommendations.

It is important during the initial planning and construction to adequately discuss and assess the future requirements for tees to ensure sufficient area is available at each hole so that tee markers can be repositioned when necessary to allow worn turf to recover quickly.

The 13th, East Course. A short hole — 135 m — in a delightful setting among gums, and seen from an elevated tee.

The official length of a golf hole is usually measured from near the back of the tee, which is indicated with a permanent mark. The turf at this distance must be formed so the markers may be moved laterally, as well as forward, for competitions that specify the full length of the course.

It is sometimes possible to establish an alternative tee at a particular hole to produce an interesting change to the playing of the hole.

A fundamental rule in constructing and maintaining tee surfaces is that they be flat and firm, and level from side to side. However, a slight fall from back to front or vice versa, for example 30mm in a distance of 3m, is not noticeable visibly, but contributes significantly to turf firmness and quality.

---

*A tee should give the impression that the flat surface already existed at the site before construction commenced; this effect is easily lost when a major effort is made to build up the whole outline.*

---

# 4

# The bunkers

Bunkers have a very important role in defining the strategy of a course, and difficulties of play are contrived by their skilful design and placement.

If there is any one array of hazardous features more than another which intrigues and generally stimulates comment from visitors to Royal Melbourne, it would assuredly be the bunkering, which is so beautifully designed on a huge scale that it is rare to find anything quite like it elsewhere. The depth of sandy soil throughout the whole area facilitated construction of such below surface features without fear of future maintenance problems arising.

The 18th, West Course, from the tee. A group of bunkers on this dog-leg to the right, with wide clear fairway on the left. The hole is 396 m – par 4.

A fairway hazard formation very often consists of mounds of varying heights with bunkers cut into them, and clearly displaying splashes of sand. They are always placed in strategic positions, for instance at the bend of a dog-leg hole, and when there is a group in this position, they are generally arranged in a slightly diagonal manner across the line of the tee shot, thus adding interest to the hole for players with varying abilities.

When the design is composed of large and impressive bunkers, the section that will cover the longest shot and the shortest route to the green must be the most conspicuous. The others in the group will be progressively lower, and with a diminishing carry from the tee, by virtue of the design following a diagonal arrangement.

In cases where a clear view of the fairway is possible, as may be obtained from an elevated tee, the inclusion of large raised features in the design of the hazard on the carry for the tee shot is generally unnecessary but if contemplated, it must be judiciously employed. The elevated tee offers an architect an opportunity to portray a fairway hazard in a less obvious manner.

It often becomes apparent while viewing well-designed groups of bunkers that forethought by the architect has made it difficult for the players to assess the extent and distance of the hazard from the tee or fairway positions.

Wherever a bunker is placed, some portion of it should be visible from the tee or fairway. Even though the only indication may be a narrow strip of sand, it should be sufficient for a player to judge the scope of the hazard as on approach.

Bunkers that are completely hidden are on occasion included in a layout, however, whether by accident or design. They should not be considered correct bunker

The 11th, East Course, 329 m. An extensive area of low mounds and hollows extends 80 m from the green. The fairway is very wide at this point. Bunkers on the right of the green are almost hidden.

planning as there is always a simple alternative of raising a mound to show an extension of the hazard.

It is essential in bunker design to try to convey a style of simplicity with the use of long sweeping curves to form an irregular outline.

While diversity is important in all aspects of golf course planning, nowhere can this be applied more aptly than in bunker design where the slightest suggestion of uniformity must be avoided. Furthermore, a group of bunkers will always appear more natural when the major axes are at relatively differing angles, thus contriving to present an impression of out-of-line formation. This latter objective is particularly important when applied to bunkers protecting greens.

The bunker and mound formation on the environs of the greens should be imaginatively designed to impart an individual character to each area.

Frequently, however, there are practical aspects that have to be considered by the architect in order to combine both natural and inspired features into the scheme.

For instance it is important to prevent storm water entering and scouring the sand on the slopes by either forming raised edges or grassy hollows in the adjacent turf to divert run-off.

The width of a bunker usually defines the maximum depth to be excavated, for example, a narrow bunker must not be too deep from a maintenance point of view, but where a certain depth is preferred it would be best to increase the width.

In situations where bunkers are exposed to strong winds, any movement of sand can be prevented to a large extent by folding the turf down slightly from the edge into the bunker on a gentle slope to enable it to be mown. This arrangement has proved in many cases to be effective and attractive in such circumstances.

Depending upon the extent and depth of a bunker, shapely turfed pathways are often necessary. As well as providing a facility for entering and leaving bunkers,

A long approach to the 14th West Course green showing an array of well-defined mounds and hollows. Bunkers on the left of the green are hidden.

Royal Melbourne East Course, the short 4th of 192 m, showing a section of a deep and expansive bunker with an island and pathways designed to reduce wind erosion.

An example of formed islands covered with dwarf native plants to assist in the prevention of wind erosion in bunkers.

they can also help to reduce wind erosion. However, the too frequent use of pathways, scallop and lobe shapes in bunker planning can only serve to divide the hazard needlessly, and, more importantly, such an outline embodied in the design could generally establish an exaggerated effect.

Bunkers that cover large expanses of sand often present a problem with wind erosion. This may be overcome to a large extent by the formation of islands raised about 15 cm above the floor and planted with a slow growing dwarf type of ground cover, other than grass, which will be seen finally as an appropriate addition to the hazard.

It is important with all bunker locations for satisfactory drainage arrangements to be made at the outset. Where greens are sited in low-lying situations it is usually more expedient to build up the area to include bunkers and undulations around the greens and enable satisfactory drainage to be installed.

It is possible in some situations to accelerate drainage from bunkers by forming a slight fall in the floor to permit a gentle flow to a point where the edge may be lowered, which could be additional to agricultural piping.

Bunkers are usually required to be shallow. To obtain satisfactory results with construction on a course with heavy soil, the base soil or clay should be carefully graded with a fall to a central line where the agricultural piping will be laid and extended well clear of the bunker, and the whole covered with coarse aggregate. This is followed by a layer of fine gravel and finally the whole bunker is finished off with a suitable grade and depth of 75mm of sand.

---

*Bunkers are planned for positions to impart strategic merit to holes. However, the importance of maintenance facility in the design must not be overlooked.*

---

# 5

# Putting green design

The siting of greens, tees and bunkers, and other hazards will give to the course a true value as a test and to a large extent be representative of the calibre of the course architect.

While the architect usually works from prepared detailed plans, a number of final decisions must be made in the field. It is possible as work proceeds from the plans, that the green formation may not be as envisaged, thus entailing alterations to ensure that strategic and visual effects are represented correctly. This is often

A rugged situation encountered on the way to the 6th green on the West Course at Royal Melbourne: a fine example of an expanse of native plants through the rough.

difficult to reproduce in a given situation, at the first attempt, from a plan or sketch.

An architect would firstly outline the holes accurately on a contour plan, leaving details of significant features to be illustrated to a larger scale by other means. In particular an enlarged plan of each green on a graph diagram can be most helpful. From it it is possible to calculate surface undulations through several sectional directions.

As an adjunct to each of these plans, an artist's perspective sketch of the finished green, as it would appear from the approach shot area, is always useful in depicting an approximate view of the finished work. A most practical method of representing a design is to produce models of the greens complete with bunkers, mounds etc.,

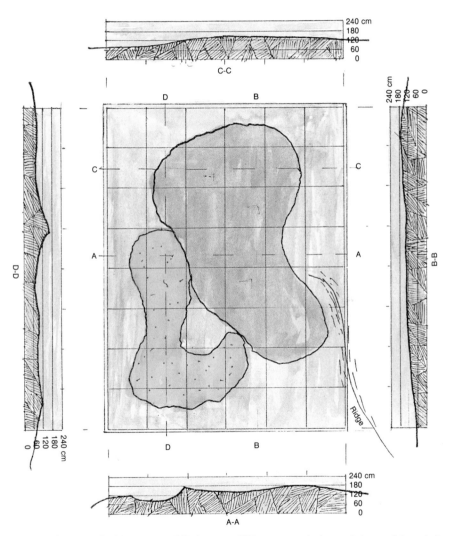

The 'Downs Country Club', proposed 3rd green, 380 m – par 4. A graph is useful to define dimensions of area and undulations.

and other characteristics planned for the environs. These may be modelled to scale clearly and accurately, showing all relevant dimensions in the plans. An ideal medium will remain in the modelled form for long periods without deterioration, and may easily be altered if necessary.

Although an architect will utilise certain methods to arrive at a result, it is what he or she sees as the designer from a position on the tee or fairway which must finally be in complete conformity with the ideas for each green.

Putting greens are of three types: first are those that are plain with little if any contouring; in others the surface characteristics are well pronounced and readily detected; in the third, however, it is the surface with a subtle rise and fall, elusive in definition, that holds a singular interest throughout a round, and which requires experience and thought by the player in deciding the line the ball will follow. This factor is, ideally, captured in the design of putting greens.

This aspect of putting green formation is noticeable at Royal Melbourne where all putts, irrespective of length or direction, must be observed and played in accord with the surface between ball and hole.

Though the immediate terrain of a site must play a significant role in the creation of the most suitable formation, and there may be several alternatives, it is essential that variations be employed to sustain interest while playing the course, each green being designed with a dissimilar aspect requiring the approach shots to be worthy of some careful thought by players.

The greens may follow a variety of shapes, and also be orientated in such a way as to allow the possibility for diverse and interesting options for play. The outlines may include a large broad back section curving towards a tapering narrow front, having some resemblance to a pear shape; an almost circular design; a general

The 17th green, West Course, showing well formed and situated undulations in front, meandering in a diagonal direction across the line of the approach shot: 416 m – par 4.

lateral slope, always an interesting alternative in the appropriate situation; or a plateau formation.

These are but a few basic ideas which, with undulating variations, may be adapted to merge into existing natural contours on a site.

Probably the most common type of green surface adopted is that which slopes from back to front. Because of its more general acceptance this style is often decided upon without sufficient consideration having been given to the natural formation of the site from which perhaps a less costly and a more interesting design may have evolved.

It is most important for a designer to recognise an appropriate area where an unusual version of a green may be constructed. An example of this nature would suggest itself, where a fairway slopes downwards to the green on a medium length two-shot hole, as being an opportunity to reverse the usual practice by forming a slight slope from front to back. In this unusual situation a green is fully visible, and the hole attracts interest as much more control is required for the approach shot.

There are several greens at Royal Melbourne with a quite unusual placement, and where the player who has taken the short line from the tee is then faced with a narrower target area because they are orientated slightly obliquely for the second shot from that line. This effect is largely influenced, and the shot made more difficult, by the intervening bunkers, and the careful positioning of the hole can form a design which contributes greatly to the merit of the course.

The green and hazards must be clearly illustrated on the plan, and also indicate that the objective of the design is to rotate the formation some degrees on its major axis.

An important part of putting green construction is to ensure with the use of mounds and hollows, that the green proper receives only its own rainfall, and not run-off from adjacent areas.

Wherever possible green formations should be divided with gentle undulations as a means of preventing water run-off following one line of flow, or a convergence of run-off meeting at one point on the green surface. There are obvious objections that relate to turf maintenance, and playing conditions, when green surfaces are such that all the flow is diverted through the centre.

Although sub-surface drainage may be adequate, it is important that excess water be cleared from a putting green surface in a reasonable time, and eventually be shed entirely. Moulding a slender curving spine into the green during construction — which can be a continuation of a mound on the verge tapering away as an almost imperceptible undulation — will provide the means to channel run-off water to two or more outlets on the perimeter of the green, a concept which when carefully done may be employed in a variety of ways to give character to putting green surfaces.

When undulations are being planned with this in mind, they will be less obvious, and thus appear more natural where the fall is minimal, and the channel follows a slightly curved line throughout its length.

In certain circumstances it is not unusual for an architect to design one or two greens in a layout with quite definite undulations forming steeper slopes; such forms are always difficult to create without having an exaggerated appearance. They can often involve arduous maintenance and extra time in putting out, and therefore must be considered carefully from the long-term point of view, before completion of the work.

When closely examined, the ideal arrangement of mounds and hollows may

Gentle and interesting undulations of the surface of a green.

invariably be seen to meander from a high point off the green, forming gentle features along its way before ultimately disappearing entirely some distance into the putting surface.

Putting green turf is expected to be of the highest standard, so it is essential to follow certain basic principles during the original construction work. The reason there are difficulties in some cases in maintaining a reasonable standard of turf can in part be determined as deriving from this initial phase. At this time precautions must be taken to calculate falls in the base soil should its permeability be in question. In a situation of this kind it is advisable to install agricultural piping in the usual manner and spread 12 mm gravel 50 mm thick over the area, followed by a minimum depth of good quality top soil to avoid the hole-cutter making contact with the gravel.

The whole question of providing conditions for optimum grass growth on the greens must be inevitably linked with soil quality, soil drainage, and finally the formation of the surface.

The surfaces of the greens may be established to approximate levels with machines, but avoiding the use of heavy vehicles on the actual green site, and leaving the essential and final contouring to be accurately completed by handwork. Care at this stage is important to ensure that the soil is evenly consolidated throughout the surface, avoiding extreme measures which may effect the soil structure, a situation which can contribute to future sustained turf grass problems.

Following the initial establishment of turf, water penetration is usually relatively free. Beyond this, however, as top-dressing is applied and firmness develops with maturity of the turf, porousness will decrease to some extent, which again serves to indicate the importance of efficient surface drainage.

When this recommendation is not adhered to, problems in turf health will arise that are difficult to overcome. These will be the result of in-built surface shortcoming which permit ponding after rain or irrigation, and which must finally be rectified for the turf to be restored to health.

---

*Putting greens are designed with discernment such as will influence the playing of the hole by those with varying standards of skill.*

---

# 6

# Drainage

Effective drainage of excess water from soil is essential where plants are to be propagated. In most circumstances when soil is cultivated surplus water moves downwards and away from the root zone. In the case of turfed areas, however, taking measures during construction for the quick removal of excess water from all types of playing surfaces is vital. Drainage can be achieved in various ways to enable play to continue or proceed without undue delay in conditions that are as near normal as possible after rainfall, or artificial watering.

In most cases which involve large sports grounds it is necessary to utilise both surface fall and an underground piped system to achieve the desired results. Playing surfaces for tennis and bowls, for instance, are required to be level, and this necessitates special sub-surface drainage arrangements in the early stages of construction. Although football and cricket grounds are required to be basically level, they are in fact usually constructed with minimum surface fall in all directions from the centre as well as having an extensive underground system of drainage.

Drainage requirements for golf courses are basically similar, and are of paramount importance in the successful propagation of turf.

During construction of fairways any natural undulations are usually retained, enlarged or developed as special features, which when completed must be mowable and self-draining.

Because of the extensive nature of golf courses, it is quite common to find certain low areas in the layout that are subject to drainage problems that require the installation of pipes, or other remedial measures, to maintain reasonable playing conditions in the affected areas. However, the opportunity to create ponds in low areas on the course that have the potential for development into attractive landscape features should not be overlooked.

Some golf courses are situated almost wholly on sandy soil which is subject to few drainage problems. On the other hand, it is important when dealing with less porous soils to ensure that as far as possible all hollows are self-draining.

If a surface fall is feasible over an area where an agricultural piping scheme is being determined, then that area should be carefully graded to assist water movement from the surface to reduce the load imposed on the pipes during storms, or at any other time when an early return to normal playing conditions is essential.

For a drainage scheme to be efficient, water must be able to flow and discharge without restriction into a larger pipe or catchment.

Sealed jointed piping is the only efficient method of collecting and moving storm-water underground to discharge at a specified point, and avoid flooding over a specific area.

Should it be necessary to install agricultural piping on land adjacent to a main pipe line, the discharge may be disposed of through openings made in the top of the large pipe. As an alternative, agricultural piping may be laid at the same level and on each side of the main pipe line, following the gradient exactly. In this instance, if it is calculated that 100mm piping will cope with the flow, then the lateral lines of piping laid to drain the surrounding turf may be 76mm diameter, entering the top of the larger pipe at each junction.

The trenches for agricultural piping should be excavated to a grade of from 0.5 per cent, and up to 2.0 per cent, denoted with pegs fixed at 3 m intervals.

A straight-edge should be used to form an exact base for the pipes to follow. Any difficulty experienced with the base of the trench can be overcome by a layer of coarse sand on which to bed the pipes.

There are several types of piping available for sub-surface drainage. The oldest forms manufactured from clay are often called tiles, and are available in 50mm, 76mm, 100mm, and 150mm diameter sizes. Of more recent manufacture are several types of plastic and polythene, with either slots or small holes provided for the entry of water throughout their entire length. Both kinds are effective, and being in long lengths, the work can be completed in less time than it takes to lay clay piping.

Although manufactured in smaller sizes than other agricultural piping, it is claimed the plastic piping removes water as effectively as other types because of the numerous points of entry. It has the additional advantage of being flexible.

A recent innovation consists of a nylon membrane or covering for plastic agricultural piping. It is claimed it effectively prevents the entry of sand, thus obviating silting of the pipes, without restricting in any way the removal of excess water.

Clay pipes require to be spaced 9.5mm apart and a strip of hessian 76mm wide placed over each joint and tucked around as far as possible to prevent the entry of fine material. Hessian is far more satisfactory for this purpose than an impervious material. Although it decays, the gravel around the piping retains its form for years.

Since the essential purpose of agricultural sub-surface drains is to remove excess water effectively, and since this is achieved only when the water is able to enter the clay pipes through the joints, spacings are vital. Because the clay absorbs moisture and expands, the space can close if the pipes are laid too closely together.

Wherever a junction occurs between lateral, semi-main, and main drains, the minor line should be arranged to enter the top of the pipe in each case, and be carefully protected at the junction with hessian.

To facilitate water movement into any agricultural drain laid in turf the pipes must be covered with material such as coke waste, coarse gravel, or screenings to within 10cm of the surface, and consolidated without undue force. This is followed by a layer of coarse sand, then soil upon which the turf may be firmly relaid.

Spacing of the main drainage lines depends largely upon the severity of the problem, which is often related to the type of soil involved. However, 12–15 m apart following a herringbone pattern is usually satisfactory.

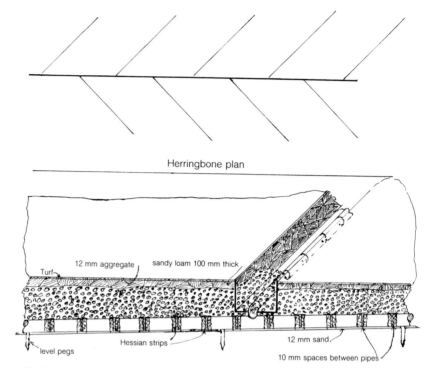

Herringbone plan

12 mm aggregate    sandy loam 100 mm thick

Turf

Hessian strips

level pegs

12 mm sand

10 mm spaces between pipes

Section of trench showing a lateral line entering top of large pipe by way of a 90° bend

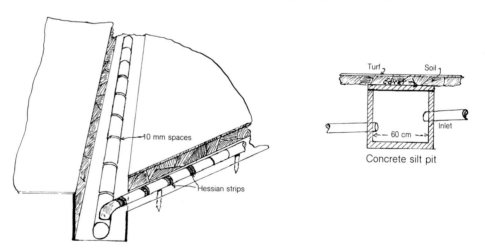

10 mm spaces

Hessian strips

Turf    Soil

cover

Inlet

← 60 cm →

Concrete silt pit

Drainage with agricultural piping.

As far as possible lines should be straight, or in long gentle curves where any change in direction is necessary, always avoiding abrupt angles.

The angle of the laterals to the main drains is usually about 45 degrees, laid where they will most effectively intercept any excess water.

It is difficult to be specific about the depth of agricultural piping for draining an area of turf as this depends largely on the fall to the outlet, which may possibly be an established storm-water drain. It is desirable, however, to have a minimum of 30cm of cover above the pipes at any point, and any clay or hardpan must be removed where necessary to maintain the correct base level for the pipes.

Depending upon the contours of the area, a change of grade in the trenches is acceptable. This can often avoid some unnecessary excavating, provided adequate fall is maintained on any section of the line.

After a number of years in operation, agricultural piping gradually loses its effectiveness through silting, especially on lines laid to a minimum fall. When this situation arises the pipes will need to be inspected and the obstruction cleared. This problem, and its correction, may be alleviated by installing silt pits 80–100 m apart which would require cleaning periodically.

Care must be taken to ensure that all pipe junctions are fully reinforced and protected, as it is at these points that most problems with flow arise.

The durability of clay agricultural pipes has been well proven over many years of use, unlike the case of polythene and plastic piping where this point has not yet been demonstrated.

It is always more economical to install drains at the time of construction, after the formation has been completed, and before planting commences. However, it is very often not possible to assess the situation, or the extent of the drainage requirements, until later when the turf is established.

The installation of drainage in turfed areas should only be attempted when the ground is firm and moist but not dry. This will offset any delays, such as those caused by wet or waterlogged conditions. The use of a sod cutter for removing established turf for the pipe trenches facilitates the work and allows a neat finish, with a quick recovery over the whole project.

As discussed in chapter 5, there are essential steps involved in the design and construction of putting greens which will contribute to optimum drainage without which the production of good durable turf becomes a very frustrating task.

Usually putting greens are built up above the natural levels with soil from an outside source, or from soil available from construction activities elsewhere on the course. Should the on-site soil have a substantial clay content, it will be necessary to use this soil to form a base, with a definite fall to the outside, before any special top soil is deposited.

Where a property has a good depth of sandy soil there are seldom any drainage problems. On the other hand, a heavy type of soil would have to be modified by the addition of some humus-forming material, coarse sand and possibly lime to give it permeability. Although such extensive modifications can be costly they lessen any possibility of future problems by providing better porosity, with increasing bacterial activity as the organic matter slowly breaks down. (See also chapters 7 and 5.)

Much of the stress which often develops in fine turf some time after it has been established can be traced to the use of an inferior top soil which does not drain satisfactorily. The retention of excess water leads to compaction, disease and turf wear.

Irrespective of soil type, it is essential that putting greens are formed to provide complete and exact surface drainage. When other than a porous sandy soil is involved, sub-surface drainage is beneficial, and becomes a fundamental requirement if the green site is likely to be affected in any way by seepage from adjacent land.

Sub-surface drains should be installed when the formation is almost complete, before any soil amendment takes place, and when drainage arrangements can be correctly assessed according to the needs of each individual design.

Consolidation of soil bulk during construction is most important as it provides stability. The formation of depressions in the turf surface often originate at the base level, later transferring to the surface with consequent ponding. However, consolidation must be judiciously carried out so that permeability of the soil is assured.

# 7

# Importance of the soil

Soil exists in a wide range of types, almost all of which provide sustenance for some form of plant life. In common with most other plants, turf grasses grow best in a soil which embodies a particular mineral particle size that relates to texture, and an organic content that will influence nutrient availability, porosity and moisture retention.

To propagate a particular plant, it is often necessary to modify the soil to correct an imbalance, and essential to cultivate it accordingly to provide an optimum medium that will supply all the elements required for its development.

Grass plants for forming turf are relatively small so obviously they must be numerous in a given area, and be aggressive enough to persistently produce new stems. Where more than one species is involved they must be selected for their ability to ultimately form turf with a close consistent character. Any species that is likely to dominate should be avoided.

A prerequisite of soil for the establishment of fine turf grass must be its capacity to withstand relatively concentrated traffic under varying conditions. Putting green turf in particular will be subject to long-term stress of many kinds, therefore the soil's physical characteristics should enable the plants to stand up to such demands over the years.

Turf maintenance difficulties that often arise later may be attributable, in part at least, to a deficiency in the physical structure of the soil used in the initial work, a defect which could possibly have been corrected at the time. Where putting green turf has been established on an appropriate foundation, it continues to retain all the desirable qualities over many years, without the decline in vigour or texture which could warrant its replacement. On the other hand, when the turf has matured, structural changes may occur which will lead to a decrease in soil porosity and drainage properties, thus seriously affecting the health of the grasses.

The composition of the soil at some golf courses leaves little to be desired, being of a sandy and fertile nature with adequate porosity. In other cases a more suitable soil has to be imported at some expense, for the putting greens at least, to use alone or be mixed with the existing soil to provide an optimum foundation for the grass. Soil tests should be arranged at the outset, however, as not all sandy soils are ideal.

During green construction, if the top-soil is found to be deficient in humus or calcium, or is too fine in texture, the condition may be corrected by the addition of some form of organic matter, such as rice hulls or brewery waste, and lime (should this be indicated by a soil test), and a quantity of very coarse sand, all of which may be spread over the surface and thoroughly incorporated into about 75mm of the top-soil by rotary hoeing.

In subsequent maintenance, it is equally important that soil for top-dressing be carefully evaluated. However, once putting green turf has been finally established, any attempt towards soil improvement by cultivation must necessarily be of a minor nature, to avoid any significant disruption of the surfaces.

Efficient surface and sub-surface drainage are of basic importance, and contribute largely towards preventing any breakdown in the physical properties of the soil. When drainage becomes less effective, particularly surface drainage, the soil may compact as a result of adverse wet weather, combined with the over-use of water during the summer, sustained play and the operation of machinery. At the same time there has to be a practical relationship, sometimes difficult to establish, between efficient drainage, and the necessary physical properties that will retain sufficient soil water to provide ideal conditions for nutrient availability and healthy durable turf on the one hand, and avoid excessive soil moisture or aridity on the other.

Just as necessary as effective putting green construction is the development of well-turfed fairways, and where sandy or loam soils are involved there is little difficulty. However, there are many courses where the basic soil is far less adaptable for growing turf, and improvement by other methods may require several years of careful management before better playing conditions become apparent.

Volcanic soils, although lacking in porosity, are very fertile and will produce good fairway turf, but must be watered when necessary to avoid drying out, which will result in shrinkage and open cracking. Wherever possible the surface should be carefully graded to prevent ponding resulting from watering or natural rainfall.

Difficulties are often experienced in establishing fairways on land where the surface soil very thinly over-lays clay, and is usually infertile. This latter deficiency must be improved with light applications of fertiliser twice yearly. After a reasonable cover of grass has been promoted top-dressing with sandy loam soil in the early spring for several years should create better playing conditions. However, the main factor for success in such circumstances is the availability of water for use over the summer. The sprinklers in this instance should be fitted with medium-size jets to avoid any heavy discharge. Short periods of irrigation, which will be sufficient to retain the moisture without flooding, are preferable.

Initially, it would be most beneficial to lightly scarify before applying any top-dressing soil. Regular light applications of fertilisers are required to maintain growth which should be mown at a height consistent with a good turf cover.

It has often been suggested that the number of years fine turf has been in play can alone be responsible for any impairment to the soil structure, but this cannot be accepted entirely because of the other important factors related to maintenance.

The keeping of full and accurate records of fine turf maintenance can provide a useful guide to possible procedures to deal with problems that may arise over the long term.

# Part two

## Turf production and maintenance

Fine turf culture, particularly in golf course work, is an absorbing study full of challenges. It is interesting to note, when comparing early turf research journals with current publications, how complex the references have become in relation to the analysis of problems, particularly those involving fine turf.

It became apparent in the 1920s, in both the UK and the USA, that research, and training for key personnel, were essential to a rapidly expanding field of industry. Participants' demands for better quality conditions were also a significant factor. It is important that research should continue on the broadest possible basis, in this country as well as overseas, to explain and overcome the many difficulties that constantly exercise the attention of leaders in the industry.

On a golf course, three types of turf are maintained: putting greens, teeing areas and fairways. Each requires special qualities for its purpose. The turf recommended for putting greens should have a firm surface, a fine texture, and be closely mown. It is composed of selected grasses, the latter being of prime importance. A true, firm surface is difficult to maintain where the turf is dense and over-stimulated, with possibly a level of thatch (this will be discussed in chapter 23).

Where there is sustained heavy play, as often occurs on pay-as-you-play and holiday season courses, the general maintenance program necessarily differs to enable the turf to endure the conditions. So although firmness remains a requisite, it is essential to sustain a more vigorous growth pattern, and mow to a higher level.

The turf for tees must consist of strong, vigorously growing grasses, which when mown will provide a pleasing level surface with the ability to quickly out-grow divot marks, involve sufficient area to permit play to take place all year round, and avoid excessive damage occurring to the turf at any time.

# 8

## Sowing grass seed

There are occasions in every turf manager's experience when new turf must be produced from seed, or maybe over-seeding old turf undertaken to overcome a state of debility. It is therefore of special significance that the person in charge is able to produce turf from seed; in fact, proficiency in providing a good surface in the shortest possible time, especially in the case of putting greens, is usually an indication of general competence.

Initial preparations are most important for the propagation and stability of turf with durable qualities. Firstly, it must be decided from a practical point of view, which time will be most suitable for sowing — spring or autumn.

If the project planning will allow a choice, then the autumn in Victoria will prove the most satisfactory. Early March, or following the first autumn rain, usually provides conditions of optimum ground temperature and moisture in which germination will be quicker than from a springtime sowing. Also, in the autumn the seedlings will develop in the mild days ahead without being exposed to extreme temperatures, and if the preparations have been carried out in correct sequence, a well-covered turf should result before the cold days of winter.

The area to be sown should be carefully formed to the planned contours, whether it be for a green, tee or fairway. In the case of a green, the top 150mm should be selected sandy soil. It would be desirable to sterilise this soil, several days prior to sowing, only if weed plants are likely to germinate. A close examination of the soil and its origin may very well indicate that sterilisation is not warranted.

After the soil on the green has been evenly consolidated, and shaped to the approved contours and levels, it is a good plan to use a 0.9 m top-dressing scraper as a final precaution in establishing an appropriate surface for mowing. The resultant formation should then be viewed from all directions to ascertain that the features are exactly as planned before proceeding with the sowing.

Surface drainage is significant in its relation to the future quality of the turf, and must receive special attention before sowing commences.

It is always advisable to establish the pH of the top soil, and should lime be required it must be applied immediately, raked deeply into the soil and watered, and after a two day lapse followed by an application of pre-sowing fertiliser consisting of 1 part nitrogen, 2 parts superphosphate, and 1 part muriate of potash at a rate of 20 g per sq m which should also be raked and watered into the soil.

Three days later the seed bed may be prepared by carefully raking straight furrows in one direction and sowing the seed immediately afterwards, either with a light distributor or by hand broadcasting. It is always necessary, particularly with the latter method, to mix the seed with screened moist sand to act as a carrier and ensure accurate distribution. As a further means of ensuring correct sowing, trials with the method to be adopted should be carried out off the site preparatory to the actual sowing operation.

A mixture of 3 of sand to 1 of seed by volume is usually satisfactory for both methods; by dividing the total mix into 2 equal parts and distributing each in a different direction over the surface, even distribution will be assured.

To cover resowing of any damage which may occur to the surface before the turf is established, put aside 2 per cent of the seed of any project before mixing.

After distribution is completed, the area must then be carefully raked in straight lines at right angles to the seed bed furrows, being careful to avoid covering the seed too deeply. The sown area should then be rolled with a lightweight roller, once only, followed by watering as required, always using a hand-held fine-spray nozzle to maintain moisture. Special attention to water requirements is vital in order to prevent drying out of any part of the sown area. Usually it is preferable to water inwards from the perimeter of the area, walking over the watered part until the entire surface is thoroughly covered.

At this stage it is often necessary to lightly cover with screened soil any seed showing on the surface, where it is considered to be excessive. If possible any further rolling should be avoided.

Grass seed as supplied by the merchants is of a very high quality, which provides a high percentage of germination and purity as a result of laboratory testing and excellent cleaning methods. However, it is not possible to achieve as high rate of germination in the field as recorded in the tests, but if care is taken it should be reasonable to expect to produce a sward to within 10 per cent of the figure stated.

It is always wise to record for future reference all relevant details of each sowing, such as date, the type and quantity of seed, fertilisers applied and weather conditions.

The seeds, when sown as recommended, are very close together and each has enough food stored within itself to start a root system and to send a shoot through the surface, provided soil moisture and a degree of warmth are present. It is at this early stage of germination that the growth process is most vulnerable to any change from a moist to a dry environment, a situation which would be detrimental to the seedlings.

When the grass is about 25–30mm high, chlorosis (or blanching) and loss of vigour may be noticed, a condition which can be corrected with an application of a weak solution of nitrogenous fertiliser. It is important to ensure forward growth is maintained until the turf is fully established.

Also at this susceptible stage of growth, it is not uncommon for a fungus, pythium disease — or damping off, an apt description of the problem — to attack the seedlings, becoming obvious as the young grass quickly melts away if not treated immediately with one of the fungicides available. A more practical approach is to apply the fungicide as a preventive before sowing, repeating about ten days after germination.

Incorrect mowing techniques in the early stages of seedling growth often cause problems that restrict the progress and development of turf to a marked degree. The initial mowing of fine turf grass should take place when the longest blades are about 38mm, using a sharp lightweight machine set at a minimum height of 19mm, and gradually lowering the cutting level over a period to 10mm.

It is more satisfactory and there is less likely to be any disruption of the surface if the mowing is carried out when the grass is dry. It is also beneficial to remove the grass clippings each time.

With frequent mowing in favourable conditions the seedlings should develop and quickly form well-covered durable turf. Alternatively, if excessive growth is permitted between mowings, the turf-forming process will take much longer to evolve.

As the turf becomes mature it must be kept under close observation to ensure growth continues by applying fertiliser as required, making an early diagnosis of any suspected disease problem and applying control measures. As a further precaution a persistent insecticide with a wide range of control should be applied against pests, which although not apparent, may be developing in the soil to cause damage later.

Where unsterilised soil has been used for the seed-bed, weeds and coarse grass species may become quite a problem in new work, because an ideal situation has been created for any unwanted plants to germinate with the grasses. These must be recognised and controlled as quickly as possible.

The unwanted grass species are the most difficult to eradicate from among young turf grasses. One such grass in particular, often prevalent in these circumstances is *Digitaria sanguinalis* — summer grass — which, if not taken in hand at a young stage will smother much of the grass, as it has a fast growth rate.

The most effective method of controlling this weed grass in this situation is to use a narrow, sharp hand-tool to carefully remove the plants when small. Further information is provided in chapter 17.

The use of hormone weedicides on seedling turf involves some risk of damage occurring and treatment with these chemicals is best delayed until the turf reaches a more mature state.

*Cynodon dactylon* — couch grass — must never be allowed to infest fine turf. *Rumex acetosella* — sorrel — is a perennial often found in young turf, and is resistant to selective chemical sprays. However, it gradually disappears as the turf develops under normal maintenance, frequent mowing being a major factor in its control.

Although in certain cases spot spraying of some broadleafed weeds will prove satisfactory, to avoid damaging the grass near the weeds care must be exercised in preparing and applying the correct solution of weedicide.

Wherever it is intended to promote couch grass turf from seed in Victoria, the sowing must be carried out in the springtime for it to obtain the maximum benefit from the warm weather ahead. Couch grass, when sown in the right conditions and given careful attention, will make remarkable headway in one growing season. There are special hulled varieties of couch seed presently available which provide a higher germination percentage in less time from a lower rate of sowing than could be expected from ordinary seed. These are important considerations, particularly if, as often occurs, for some reason sowing has been delayed, thus reducing the initial growing season.

In the case of large areas such as fairways, some form of mechanical preparation

## Table of seed sowing for turf

### Recommended rates and mixtures for fine turf

| Botanical and common names | Recommended quantity per square metre |
|---|---|
| *Agrostis tenuis*<br>or<br>New Zealand or brown top, and a similar type of tenuis known as highland bent<br>*Festuca rubra* var. commutata<br>or<br>Chewings fescue | 14 g       } a mixture of 35 g<br>21 g |
| *Agrostis tenuis* as above | 14 g, may be used alone, suitable for any fine turf area, or home lawns. |
| *Agrostis tenuis*, as above.<br>*Agrostis pulustris*<br>or<br>creeping bent<br>*Festuca rubra*, as above | 7 g<br>7 g     } a mixture of 35 g<br>21 g |
| hybrid bent<br>or<br>penncross | 14 g |
| *Agrostis canina*<br>or<br>velvet bent | 14 g. Extremely fine grass, tends to colonise and exclude other species in a mixture. Seed not readily available. |

### Over-seeding fine turf

*Agrostis tenuis*, or alternatively    7 g
hybrid bent    7 g

### Recommended rates and mixtures for sowing tees, fairways, and similar turf

| Botanical and common names | Quantity of seed required |
|---|---|
| *Cynodon dactylon*<br>or<br>couch grass<br>*Poa pretensis*<br>or<br>Kentucky blue | 56 kg<br>      } *Fairways* A mixture of 112 kg per hectare<br>56 kg |
| *Cynodon dactylon*<br>or<br>couch grass<br>*Poa pretensis*<br>or<br>Kentucky blue | 14 g<br>      } *Tees* A mixture of 28 g per square metre<br>14 g |

of the soil and seed distribution is necessary, and a pre-sowing application of fertiliser is usually advisable. Most fertiliser distributors are adjustable to spread small amounts of fine seed accurately.

As is the case with small areas, the soil must be cultivated deeply to a fine tilth, and surface levels and contours finally established before sowing commences.

If possible, it is preferable to sow the seed, harrow lightly, and follow with a drag to cover the seed, all in a single operation rather than duplicate the use of the tractor.

Apart from employing a fertiliser distributor for sowing, as already mentioned, a method which agitates and drops the seed from the hopper to spreading boards, thence to the soil, there are also seed drills available which deposit the seed in rows, covering it in the same operation. With this type of machine, the rows must be close together with an adjustable sowing depth gauge to avoid over-covering of the seed. As a general rule, to achieve maximum germination of such small seeds, the sowing depth should be from 6–12mm in all circumstances. The importance of preventing the seed being covered too deeply, and of rolling lightly once over, are factors common to all seed sowing practices.

Broadcasting machines provide an alternative method of sowing, distributing from an impeller plate situated below the hopper, and although they do not sow as uniformly as fertiliser distributors, there are circumstances such as unstable soil where this method could prove to be the most suitable.

The methods used in overseeding established turf vary from those already noted. The necessity to over-seed existing turf may be for any one of a number of reasons; often it is considered to be the only way an improvement in turf quality may be achieved in a given time.

In the case of fine turf, a seed-bed must be provided by lightly disturbing the surface with a scarifier, and applying a weak solution of a complete fertiliser before sowing, and finally a light top-dressing of sandy soil. It is also advisable to sow an extra 10 per cent of seed above normal estimates to overcome a lower emergence rate brought about by a seed-bed which is usually much less than ideal. Furthermore, in the case of fine turf, play invariably continues without respite. These two factors are not conducive to maximum seedling development.

The most satisfactory results are obtained where temporary greens are played for a period of perhaps six weeks, allowing the young grass to reach a stage where it can withstand normal maintenance and play.

Where fairway turf is concerned, re-seeding may be necessary to restore bare or weak parts that are causing concern. The areas involved would require being lightly harrowed or raked to form a suitable seed-bed, and this followed by an application of a complete fertiliser which must be raked in and watered and left to stand for three days before sowing the seed, then finally top-dressed lightly with sandy soil.

The surface must be carefully watered before and after germination takes place. Small sections are relatively simple to maintain in this regard, whereas large seeded areas would possibly require sprinklers with a wide cover and fitted with fine discharge jets to operate in frequent changes of position to avoid water damage occurring on the surface.

Species and quantities of seed must be decided upon relative to the most desirable type of turf for the project in hand and its future use; for instance, fairway turf should consist of durable hardy grasses that possess turf-forming characteristics. A mixture which will provide these qualities may consist of couch and Kentucky blue, with the addition of Chewings fescue recommended for tees.

# 9

# Vegetative planting

The vegetative method of turf grass propagation has, over many years, been successfully employed for a variety of reasons. With care in management, mature turf true to type can be more quickly achieved by this method than by sowing the seed of the same species. The procedure also enables a small stock of a variety considered to have special turf grass characteristics to be studied and researched in a small plot, or it may be gradually increased by division to form a larger turfed area for some other activity.

This method of planting is often used on slopes in preference to sowing seed where there is a risk of erosion occurring through wind or water; in this situation the furrows for planting the stock should run across the slopes.

Although turf maturity is reached earlier, the labour costs involved to complete a project of any size would be higher than for seeding an area of similar size. In the first place the selected stock has to be lifted, separated into small pieces and, most importantly, all the soil removed before planting.

Soil preparations are similar to those prescribed for seeding, and when completed, pieces of rooted stock must then be planted close together in shallow furrows 100mm apart, lightly rolled to make firm, and top-dressed with sandy soil, making sure to leave a small portion of each plant protruding.

When a large-scale project of this nature is under consideration arrangements must be made to prevent the stock deteriorating after it has been dug from the ground. Usually if left in bulk for any length of time heat will be generated with consequent loss of viability. Therefore, it should be spread out in the shade, and watered when necessary to keep it fresh until planted.

When long distances from the source of supply are involved, and to avoid any set-back to the stock en route, refrigerated transport or similar precautions may be necessary to ensure that stock reaches the site in a fresh condition.

Turf of putting green standard may be cultivated by the vegetative planting method provided sufficient stock is known to be available. It is more satisfactory, where such large important areas are concerned, to shred or chaff the stock and broadcast a thin layer over the surface, then lightly roll and top-dress with dry screened soil, using a light fertiliser distributor for the purpose.

In common with any other planting-out project, the soil must be moist to begin with; springtime is the optimum season for planting creeping bent or couch grass roots, as from then progressive growth may be expected through the autumn.

Timing of the initial mowing is important, and should be executed with a well adjusted machine set at a level that will only remove any upright growth and not cut into, or disturb the plants in any way, as careful mowing at this stage will encourage stolon growth.

The grasses most adaptable to vegetative planting are those with rhizomes and stolons such as the bents and couch species. For best results when establishing an area of turf from creeping bent or couch grass, it is recommended that they be planted separately rather than in combination. When couch is to be planted in this way, deep cultivation of the soil is important to promote and sustain vigorous growth in the future.

*Cynodon transvaalensis* — commonly called fine couch — is a very fine South African couch grass with an aggressive habit, and can be expected to make excellent progress under favourable summer conditions from vegetative planting, and once established it has a tendency to exclude other grasses, and retain a brown colour during the period it is dormant in Victoria. Initially, a small quantity of this grass was introduced into Australia about 1930, and although it has never been available commercially, it has been dispersed, and can now be found growing in small areas in many parts of the country.

In the USA experiments with *Cynodon dactylon* and *Cynodon transvaalensis* have produced several superior hybrids with the characteristics of both species. These are available commercially and planted extensively in America wherever conditions are suitable. Research in Australia tends increasingly towards developing native grasses.

Prior to the development of present-day mechanisation, which has resulted in a remarkable diversity of efficient golf course equipment, many of the older fairways on golf courses around Melbourne were established by planting couch roots vegetatively, and now after more than fifty years, this excellent turf is still vigorous, continuing to provide wonderful playing conditions.

Projects of this nature were large and extended undertakings, the total area to be planted out on eighteen holes being approximately 15 hectares. Although such a procedure would not be economically possible today, there is no doubt that, with all the sophisticated means of cultivation presently available, a far less arduous and efficient method for planting fairways could be evolved if ever the occasion arose.

Further information concerning vegetative planting is noted in chapter 16.

# 10

## Fertilisers and turf production

Turf can be defined as specially cultivated grasses, which require surface applications of fertilisers periodically, in either dry or liquid form.

When deciding upon a fertiliser, the analysis needs to be fully understood to ensure that the constituents are in a ratio that will provide the greatest benefit to both the soil and the grass plants. The choice of a fertiliser must also take into account at all times the expected period of response, and whether the result will provide a firm and durable turf.

Intensive culture of putting green turf is often regarded as essential, and although to some degree this is true, it should not be taken to mean that frequent applications of excessive quantities of nitrogenous fertilisers are required to produce the type of turf described.

It is most important, however, that the top-dressing procedures as recommended for greens be carried out on a regular basis, and the requirements of the turf at other times of the year be assessed individually, and not to a pre-arranged over-all fertiliser schedule. Such a policy could mean that while the turf may be less subject to stress, growth is being over-stimulated.

Frequent brushing and combing are important factors in producing a good texture, and when performed in conjunction with the judicious use of fertilisers excellent putting surfaces will result, as opposed to thick verdant turf which is less durable and lacks that desirable quality which can reveal putting finesse. Turf colour is not a prerequisite for a good putting surface.

Concentrated fertiliser solutions consisting of major elements alone, or alternatively, with the addition of micro nutrients, may, in the case of small areas, be applied under mains water pressure, through syphon or venturi type fittings, or with a power-operated system, after adding a volume of water to the recommended quantity of the fertiliser.

There are a number of comparable dry fertiliser mixtures available, and as a rule the manufacturer will be prepared to vary a mix to the customer's specification, with minor nutrients if required. This may be applied by broadcasting, mixed with top-dressing soil, or if the components are immediately soluble, by a spraying method.

Caution may be necessary in some localities regarding the frequency with which minor elements are applied, as they are required by plants in minute and rather exact quantities, and any excess in certain conditions may contribute to some future turf problem.

A good plan with a fertilising program is to arrange to apply suitable alternative mixtures rather than continue using one combination of elements, particularly if micro nutrients are involved.

Of the major elements, nitrogen is the most essential, and is indispensable in the propagation of fine turf grass. In this area the quantities and frequency of applications must be judged by observation, and always with the object of maintaining a uniform and steady growth, which is often achieved by applying less than the basic quantity.

A balanced fertilising program is essential for the successful cultivation of good fine turf on a year-to-year basis. The elements applied are decomposed by bacterial action in the soil to a form where they can be taken up by the plants, and must include units of organic and inorganic fertilisers.

A fraction is leached away with water movement, and chemical analyses have shown that grass clippings contain a percentage of all nutrients applied. Nevertheless the removal of grass is recommended and there are few exceptions to this rule when mowing fine turf.

Phosphorus is another major element and is mainly supplied through applications of superphosphate in various mixtures. An available supply is essential for sound root development and other vital growth processes, and in most instances sufficient is provided to meet this need if applied in the relatively small amounts recommended in the top-dressing schedules.

Potassium, also a major element, is available from the manufacturer as sulphate or muriate, and should always be accessible to the grass plants. For some years it has been observed in practice that, when used regularly in combination with ammonium sulphate and superphosphate as a complete fertiliser, it has the effect of producing more durable and healthier turf with some resistance to disease.

The three major elements noted are obtainable in varying proportions in solution or in dry mixtures, or they may be procured separately in dry form and mixed by the purchaser. The liquid formulations are simple to use on the site. By applying slightly less than the manufacturer's recommendation for fine turf, it is possible to promote a satisfactory response. On the other hand, any dry mix fertiliser requires care to avoid scorching after-effects when applying it to fine turf. It should therefore be pre-mixed with screened sand to facilitate even distribution, and watered immediately after application. (Further information regarding dry mixtures is noted in chapter 12.)

The inorganic nitrogen applied to turf is generally obtained from ammonium sulphate (nitrogen content 21%) or urea (nitrogen content 46%). A quantity of urea, therefore, will supply twice as much nitrogen as an equivalent amount of ammonium sulphate. However, there is a noticeable difference in the type of growth produced by each of the two fertilisers.

The effect obtained from ammonium sulphate is longer lasting, and the growth more durable than that derived from urea, which tends to react more quickly, and produce growth of a less hardy nature which is often prone to disease. However, when urea is included in a mixture in comparatively small amounts as set out in the 'Fertiliser recommendations' tables on pages 52–3, it becomes an accessory of an excellent combination of fertilisers suitable for fine turf.

It is recognised that repeated applications of nitrogenous fertilisers are necessary

## Table of fertiliser recommendations

| Greens | |
|---|---|
| December 21<br>March 20 | **Summer**<br>Apply only when necessary.<br>A complete liquid fertiliser at less than the manufacturer's recommendation, with the addition of two grams Iron Sulphate per square metre. Alternatively, a dry mixture consisting of:<br>Sulphate of ammonia    10 g<br>Urea    4 g    per sq m,<br>Muriate of potash    4 g    applied in solution<br>Iron sulphate    2 g |
| March 21<br>June 20 | **Autumn**<br>If required apply either of the above mixtures, having regard to the top-dressing program due at this time. Refer to chapter 12 for the recommended quantities of fertiliser. An application of a complete liquid fertiliser about six weeks after top-dressing may be necessary to maintain progressive growth through the winter. |
| June 21<br>September 20 | **Winter**<br>A further application of fertiliser if required over this period, consisting of:<br>Sulphate of ammonia    14 g<br>Urea    4 g    per sq m,<br>Muriate of potash    5 g    applied in solution<br>Iron sulphate    2 g |
| September 21<br>December 20 | **Spring**<br>Refer to the spring top-dressing recommendations. When required, a complete liquid fertiliser as advised for the summer quarter may prove beneficial if applied late November. The liquid fertiliser suggested should contain approximately,<br>Nitrogen    15%<br>Phosphorus    3%<br>Potash    5% |

to maintain turf grass in an acceptable condition for play, but it is also desirable that the quality of a fine turf area be appraised before any fertiliser application, with the object of retaining a moderate top growth with a minimum of fertiliser. By avoiding over-stimulation of putting green turf in this way, lower maintenance usually results, and the grasses reproduce effectively over a longer period.

Organic nitrogen is released slowly in the course of decomposition, therefore the effects are longer lasting. The same benefits become available through this process when any of the natural waste materials, which also carry moderate amounts of other essential growth elements, have been incorporated into top-dressing soil, or used as a pre-sowing soil amendment in association with inorganic fertilisers.

Iron sulphate is an essential trace element involved in the formation of chlorophyll in plants, and is one which may be applied to fine turf in larger amounts with significant results. It is obtainable in a soluble calcined form, and added to fertilisers in wet or dry applications.

The root system of fine turf grass will benefit noticeably from an application of *Formula 20* in the spring and autumn, either alone, or added to a liquid fertiliser.

| Tees | |
|---|---|
| December 21<br>March 20 | **Summer**<br>Normal seasonal growth should continue as a result of earlier applications, providing irrigation has been carried out when required. |
| March 21<br>June 20 | **Autumn**<br>A dry application of 2–2–1, applied at 28 g per sq m, and watered into turf. |
| June 21<br>September 20 | **Winter**<br>To maintain vigorous growth over this period, apply in solution a mixture of:<br>Calcium ammonium nitrate  20 g<br>Muriate of potash              7 g     per sq m |
| September 21<br>December 20 | **Spring**<br>A dry application of 2–2–1, similar to the autumn recommendation, followed by a soil top-dressing. Should it become necessary to maintain growth, a similar mixture as prescribed for the winter period may be applied at any time during the year. |

| Fairways | |
|---|---|
| | **Summer and winter**<br>It is an advantage on some golf courses to apply fertiliser to the fairway turf in the spring and autumn. In other situations it is sufficient to fertilise in the spring only. The summer and winter are not usually included in these recommendations. |
| March 21<br>June 20 | **Autumn**<br>An application of complete fertiliser, 2–2–1, applied at 225 kg per hectare. |
| September 21<br>December 20 | **Spring**<br>A mixture of:<br>Calcium ammonium nitrate  6 parts<br>Superphosphate              1 part<br>Muriate of potash              2 part<br>Applied at 225 kg per hectare.<br>This mixture should be used as soon as possible, and not stored for any length of time. |

It is imperative for the turf manager to be fully aware of the pH reaction of all relevant soil and understand the changes that may occur to this value as a result of any planned application of fertilisers. Soil-testing kits are obtainable and are useful in providing an approximate pH reading, but a report obtained from an appropriate authority would be far more informative, and should be requested once every two years.

*Poa annua* is a grass that is a scourge of fine turf throughout the world, and has the ability to thrive in a varying range of soil conditions, from comparative nutrient poverty through a high degree of soil fertility. In the production of fine turf, it is often encouraged to grow vigorously and multiply through certain components in composite fertilisers, a situation where a putting surface is impaired, and control measures can become unreliable and frustrating. (For further information refer to chapter 21.)

In most localities fairway turf would benefit from regular fertiliser treatment once each year; in other cases spring and autumn applications may often be necessary to maintain durable turf.

It is important at all times to take into account the composition of the fertiliser and the rate at which the mixture is to be applied, in association with the prevailing state of the turf, to ensure the continuance of a moderate growth, as opposed to an over-invigorated effect which may well be less enduring.

The fairway fertiliser would also be suitable for the teeing areas, although more frequent applications may be necessary to promote forward growth that will assist in the quick recovery of divot marks.

Whenever fertilisers are distributed on golf course turf, either wet or dry, it is important to employ accurate methods, thereby contributing significantly to the final effect. Irrespective of the method adopted, accuracy implies efficient dispensing at the source in conjunction with some form of indicator which will enable the operator to avoid over- or under-covering of the turf during travel, which would be seen later as distributing errors. Of the distributing methods available, centrifugal broadcasting is the most difficult with which to obtain accuracy, because of the wide cover.

Because the fertiliser is intended to specifically encourage growth only on the fairways proper, on no account must it be permitted to flow on to the adjoining rough cut. This is difficult to avoid with a broadcaster.

The maximum benefit will be derived from fertilisers applied to fairway turf when a moderate rainfall follows. Alternatively, if irrigation is operative and dry weather follows distribution, the turf should be watered as it is possible otherwise to lose a percentage of certain elements into the atmosphere. Fertilisers should not be applied to fine turf that is in a dry condition. To avoid harmful after-effects occurring in these circumstances, the turf would need to be well watered before and after the application.

Analyses of fertilisers, quantity applied, date of applications, the result obtained, and the weather conditions should all be recorded for future reference.

Fertilisers should never be allowed to remain in a distributor overnight as they are liable to absorb moisture from the atmosphere and consolidate, or partially liquefy. Mechanical distributors should always be thoroughly cleaned after use, especially in the case of dry materials which cause serious corrosion when left in contact with metal parts. Maintenance should consist of dismantling, wire-brushing, and washing off all traces of fertiliser then finally painting all metal parts with oil, before storing away under cover. Clean water forced through a liquid distributor system after use should be sufficient to prevent deterioration. However, should corrosive action occur, it is difficult thereafter to obtain accurate distribution.

Supplies of preferred fertilisers are not always readily available, despite the fact that there have been many combinations of growth elements recently introduced, usually in commercial mixtures which are expensive and, in some cases, not entirely appropriate for fine turf culture. It would prove both convenient and economical, as future price rises appear inevitable, and providing dry storage arrangements are at hand, to stockpile to a certain extent when the required type of fertiliser is available.

# 11

## Applying lime to turf

Lime is the most economical material for correcting soil acidity and is readily available in several forms. However, the type generally recommended for turf is agricultural ground limestone.

Dolomitic limestone, because of the high magnesium content, is often recommended when a deficiency of this element has been established.

There is also available in Victoria another limestone which contains a moderate amount of potash and is frequently preferred for this reason.

Basic slag is a neutralising material, a by-product of steel manufacture with the addition of phosphoric acid, but should not be chosen for this reason as the necessary phosphate supply for turf grass is more readily available by the use of superphosphate.

These materials are required to fulfil a fineness specification in manufacture, and are suitable for application to the turf of tees and fairways.

The direct use of ground limestone to fine turf often proves difficult and unsatisfactory, whereas, if it is mixed with soil and applied as top-dressing even distribution is more readily achieved.

There is an effective and efficient super-fine lime powder available which is recommended for fine turf in particular. Because it is so finely prepared it mixes easily with water for spraying application, and is therefore quickly effective, an important consideration in respect to fine turf. It is unlike ground limestone, which contains a proportion of large particles that are slow-acting, particularly when applied to fine turf surfaces. Moreover, if the recommended quantity is high because of a low pH, it is more simple to make successive applications to fine turf by spraying than by dry distribution.

Shell lime is manufactured by crushing and grinding shells to a specified degree of fineness and has a similar analysis as that of ground limestone and acts in a like manner. It is cleaner and easier to handle than other lime, with the exception of lime powder, and for this reason is often favoured for use on small areas of turf.

Calcium is an essential element, and a form of lime presents the most practical way of introducing it to the soil when required. It has been established that the calcium supply becomes depleted as it is taken up by the plants, mainly in root development, and to a lesser extent loss occurs in the grass clippings.

There are facets of turf work where good judgement and sometimes a sixth sense are important requisites. In the area of soil reaction, however, it is essential for a turf manager to have a full understanding of the soil and the effects thereon of the various elements required to provide quality turf all year round. It is important to become informed as to why some vital nutrients are locked in, and others remain available to plants when the pH values vary beyond the figures stated below, low pH or acidity being more common to turf than an alkaline reaction.

Lime applications for the cultivation of turf should only be undertaken following a soil test by an appropriate authority, which will recommend the exact amount required to correct the acidity. It is usually advisable for a test to be carried out on a two- or three-yearly basis in the case of fine turf grass, mainly because of the regular applications of nitrogenous fertilisers.

It is essential for a turf manager to have a soil-testing kit on hand, which, with a little experience, will enable a reasonably accurate pH of the soil to be obtained at any time. Should a comprehensive analysis be considered advisable, a laboratory test is recommended.

Agrostis species (bent grasses), fescues, and Cynodon species are the grasses generally cultivated for golf course turf and are tolerant of similar pH values of 6.2–7.0. However, there have been many instances noted of excellent firm, fine bent and fescue turf in soil with a strongly acid reaction, pH 5.5, a condition in which acidity would continue to increase unless corrected with applications of lime.

It has also come to be accepted that turf grasses generally prefer a slightly acid soil condition in pH 6.0–6.5 range, which in most cases will enable healthy optimum growth to be produced under normal maintenance procedures.

It must be noted, however, that references have been made, on a practical rather than a scientific basis by sources both in Australia and overseas, that firm and finely textured turf for putting greens has been supported over very long periods by a more acid reaction, of approximately pH 5.8. This has often led to discussions for and against a specific soil condition, particularly if the more acid state enables these admirable turf qualities to be retained, and in turn, is commended by players of note and others.

Soils vary naturally from acid through neutral — 7.0 — to alkaline, and there is an effective balance between acid and alkaline materials in a soil with a neutral reaction. It is also feasible, but unlikely, to find all the necessary constituents correctly embodied in the soil of a particular district, as recommended for the propagation of fine turf. But should this ideal condition be the case initially, close attention would be required to anticipate any soil reaction change with progressive maintenance.

To avoid any possibility of injurious effects accruing when a large quantity of lime has been recommended for fine turf grass, it is usually more practical to arrive at the figure with two applications, allowing time for the first to be assimilated into the turf before proceeding.

Soon after an application of lime to a turf surface a response may become apparent. However, decomposition of the lime particles and the effect of this on the top soil to a depth of 7.5 or 10cm is a long and beneficial process, whereby microbial activity and nutrient availability are increased throughout the root area of the grasses.

It is usually possible to maintain the optimum pH, and thus avoid any significant increase in residual acidity in fine turf receiving normal applications of nitrogenous fertilisers by applying a light dressing of lime yearly, assessing this quantity from soil tests undertaken on a two- or three-yearly basis.

A soil condition in which organisms thrive plays a vital role in the retention of moisture and the movement of air in the soil. Suitable sub-surface material completes an environment for healthy turf grass growth.

Although good firm turf can be produced on a soil with a reaction below pH 5.8, which is approaching a strongly acid condition, there are usually consequential problems involved such as summer dryness, which becomes noticeable early in the season and can be extremely difficult to overcome even with the assistance of aeration. This degree of acidity can also cause noticeable retardation in the vital area of root development.

The basic ideal of fine turf grass management must be to reproduce a continuous sward using minimum quantities of growth-producing materials, which would tend to give some control over acidity, as well as other related benefits.

Because of the obvious differences in grass species and quality of fairway turf compared to fine turf grass, it is possible to apply a much greater quantity of ground limestone in one operation if necessary, without harmful effects to the turf.

A centrifugal broadcaster is the most suitable machine for distributing a heavy rate of limestone on fairway turf. Due allowance must be made along each pass for sufficient overlap to achieve uniformity as this type of machine often tends towards lighter distribution on the extremes of the spreading.

Difficulties can arise when attempting uniformity with a drop-type distributor, as the lime tends to consolidate and bridge over the agitator parts of the machine in the hopper.

When it is planned to correct a moderately acid reaction in fairway turf, an application of lime and superphosphate 1.1 will produce a significant neutralising effect. This mixture is usually available from the manufacturer, and it spreads uniformly without difficulty from either drop or broadcast distributor. The rate may be varied from 127 kg–hectare for a moderately acid pH, a higher quantity being applied when the reaction is lower than pH 6.0.

The most favourable time to apply lime to fairways is during winter and early spring.

Nitrogenous fertilisers such as ammonium sulphate or urea are acid forming, while superphosphate, sulphate and muriate of potash are neutral in their reaction. Therefore it is usually the quantity of nitrogenous fertiliser applied that determines the lime required to neutralise the resultant acidity.

# 12

## Top-dressing of turf

The application of a layer of suitable soil to grass surfaces has long been known as top-dressing, and it was obvious from the response, even in earlier times, that turf derived much benefit from the practice. However, despite the fact that top-dressing is an old and proven technique, it has in some instances been overlooked as an essential procedure in fine turf maintenance, often with indifferent results.

Moreover, although the effect of regular top-dressing has usually been beneficial on the surface, frequently far too much soil is applied, contributing to excessive layering beneath the surface and to later maintenance complications. This custom may have originated in the days when turf consisted of couch and other coarse grass species which required a heavy dressing of soil in the spring, and later carried over to the fine bent turf era. With undue delay in recovery to a normal turfed surface, the practice justifiably gave rise to criticism from many players. Also this manner of top-dressing required more time than was really necessary, which may have been a further reason for management to question its validity as a means of cultivating firm putting green turf.

With the light earth-moving equipment that is available today the whole operation, if efficiently organised, may be readily undertaken and completed economically, and without inconveniencing players on the course to any extent.

Although turf maintenance practices differ, there is no substitute for correct top-dressing procedures, particularly where fine turf is involved, and it should form part of any program where quality turf is envisaged, or for any other grade of turf for that matter. However, while the top-dressing schedule is important for the well-being of the turf, top-dressing soil recently applied should not form the putting surfaces for major events.

There are significant advantages in procuring suitable soil from the property wherever possible, since its origin and quality are known. However, most golf clubs have no other alternative than to purchase from an outside source, in which case careful selection must ensure that it is supplied from the surface and to a prescribed depth only. It is also necessary to ascertain if there are any plants growing at the site which could become problems later.

The soil must be of a sandy nature, of high porosity, and because it is surface soil would undoubtedly contain a percentage of humus, which is such an important constituent in soil for top-dressing turf.

The ideal arrangement for the undertaking is to make available a top-dressing shed with a concrete floor, large enough for a truck to deposit the soil, and for a tractor with loader to work inside at times of distribution. If a shed of such dimensions is not available, it would be advisable at least to provide an area of concrete where the soil can be prepared before application to the turf.

If possible the soil should not be screened, particularly if it contains small debris such as partially decayed leaves and roots etc., because in the process of preparation, followed by spreading and scraping over the surface, particles of this waste become incorporated with the soil, thereby allowing extra humus to be worked into the turf, leaving any larger fragments of waste to be disposed of in the final levelling process.

Where a mechanical top-dressing unit is employed the soil must be moderately dry and relatively free of debris for efficient operation.

The turf derives the greatest benefit if the operation is carried out in the spring and autumn; if circumstances prevent this, an autumn application would probably give the better result.

Prior to the work commencing the turf should be closely mown, with a brush attachment if necessary, to remove excess growth and establish a basis for a minimum requirement of soil. Nevertheless, there should always be sufficient to allow any minor irregularities in the turf surface to be properly levelled.

Should for any reason the putting surfaces ever become extremely out of character, this must be rectified gradually. It may take several applications extending over maybe a two-year period before a desirable putting surface is attained.

The object of the top-dressing procedure is to establish durable, firm and smooth putting turf by supporting the grass plants physically and organically.

Timing for the operation is important, so several days should be selected when the least number of players is expected on the course, as they seldom appreciate playing on greens in various stages of top-dressing. It is also important from a management view-point that the work is interrupted as little as possible, thus completing as many greens each day as circumstances permit, and retaining the highest degree of uniformity of recovery of the surfaces.

Should the soil be moist when applied, or a shower of rain intervene, it is essential before proceeding that time be given for it to dry to facilitate the levelling effect, and also to fulfil the basic reason for the procedure by permitting the soil particles to fall between the grass blades and stems, to the soil beneath.

The weather is always a major factor in the time taken to complete the work; fine and windy conditions are always the most favourable. Although it is always frustrating and time-consuming when unfavourable showery weather intervenes, it is most important that the work be completed properly as the weather conditions improve and the soil dries on the turf.

Under favourable conditions it is usual to spread the soil on a number of greens to allow it to become thoroughly dry before returning to the starting point to begin the scraping in, and levelling off the top-dressing with 90cm-wide bevel-edged scrapers. Similar handwork appears to be necessary following mechanical spreading of top-dressing soil, to ensure that it is thoroughly worked into the turf.

Whenever possible the final scraping operation following either mechanical or hand-spreading should be done in different directions, that is north to south in the autumn, east to west in the spring. This will reduce the tendency for imperfections to develop in the surfaces.

The top-dressing operation provides an excellent opportunity to apply fertilisers to the turf. This may be done separately, in either liquid or dry form, before applying the soil, or by pre-mixing fertilisers and soil, and leaving as a compost for a period of not less than two weeks before using. Although the former method may be adopted in certain cases where there are labour considerations to take into account, the latter method is preferred, as an early growth response can be expected because the elements in the compost become more readily available to the plants through bacterial activity.

Obviously the quantity of soil required must vary according to total area, but as a general rule, 0.8 cu m to 585 sq m of an average putting green surface may be taken as a guide, which allows for an approximate thickness of 1.5mm. By knowing the area of each green, and the total area of turf involved, the quantity of each unit of fertiliser can then be accurately estimated, irrespective of the method followed.

These quantities of dry fertilisers must be put through a 6mm-sieve and then thoroughly mixed together to enable even incorporation into the soil. The required amount of soil must be on hand to apply after liquid fertiliser applications, and also for dry fertiliser and soil mixed top-dressing.

In the latter case the soil should form a stack with regular dimensions such as 5.5 by 4.5 by 0.9 m = 20.25 cu m, which would be sufficient to treat eighteen greens, plus a practice putting green. The pre-mixed fertilisers are then spread evenly over the surface of the stack and raked into the top 10cm, followed by a complete mixing of soil and fertilisers, either by machine or handwork.

To proceed with the latter course, a conical-shaped pile is formed by shovelling on to the apex until it is about 1 metre high to eventually form a triangular prism as mixing progresses into the original stack, which should be divided to produce two such triangular formations. By continuing to shovel on to the apex the fertilisers and soil flow down over the sloping sides and become thoroughly and evenly blended.

It is always advisable to repeat the mixing process, and before actually starting the top-dressing of the greens, it is prudent to take samples with a trowel from a number of points over the whole mix, and apply the total sample to a small area of turf as a test against the possibility of contamination having occurred in some way during the preparation of the mixture.

If facilities were available that could house a double quantity of soil, mixing could then be done in advance, if necessary during inclement weather.

Any disease or weed control measures that may be indicated should be carried out before proceeding with the top-dressing.

It is important to adopt careful mowing procedures as the grasses are growing through the top-dressing. This should be at a slightly higher level than usual and without the grass-catcher, and when the surface is either well-watered or thoroughly dry, and the result will be a clean finish. If the grass-catcher is used in the early stages of regrowth, it is possible that a quantity of fertiliser will be collected from the surface before it has broken down, and thereby lost. As the grasses grow through and the surfaces have recovered sufficiently, the usual mowing procedures may be resumed.

Immediately following top-dressing, it may be necessary to move the holes more often than usual, as the tender grass shoots can quickly show signs of deterioration from traffic in the adjacent area. In addition, wherever possible the holes should be placed near the walk-off side of the green for a time, an idea that can be used whenever it is desirable to restrict the movement of the players to some degree, for the benefit of the turf.

The teeing surfaces always profit from soil top-dressing, and should be included in the spring program. In this instance it is preferable to fertilise the turf before applying the soil. Because of divot marks and the type of turf associated with tees, much more soil must be applied than is the case with fine turf to achieve and retain the requisite flat, uniform surfaces.

At first thought, the idea of top-dressing fairways with soil may seem impractical because of the magnitude of such a project. However, in the initial stages of fairway turf development, a light top-dressing with sandy soil will always prove most beneficial, particularly when applied to couch grass. Later, as the turf matures and at a time when it is possible to assemble some extra staff with the necessary soil and equipment, an effort to top-dress several fairways each spring, and so bring all the fairways within the scope of the program once every four years, would certainly be of long-term benefit.

For the successful top-dressing of any extensive area of turf the weather must be suitable, and the soil reasonably dry and clean to allow it to flow from the distributing vehicle at an acceptable thickness and thus minimise handwork, and facilitate the smoothing and levelling process, which is affected with chain harrows with a wire-netting drag attached.

For various, often obscure, reasons, it is not unusual for parts of fairways to deteriorate to a stage where renovation in some form is obviously necessary. Firstly, if the cause of the problem is known an improvement may be expected following treatment. However, should the cause remain vague, recovery can be achieved in most cases by lightly harrowing or scarifying the affected areas, followed with an application of complete fertiliser plus trace elements. A heavy top-dressing with good quality sandy soil is the next and most beneficial operation, before finally raking and reseeding the area.

# 13

---

# Irrigation of turf grass

---

Although there are fewer players using golf courses during the summer, it is nevertheless a very busy and arduous period for the curator. The maintenance of fine turf during the warm weather presents specific difficulties because, although each season has its quirks, no other period of the year requires so much concentrated effort to retain the overall good health of fine turf as the summertime. In the Victorian climate watering care is necessary from late spring through early autumn, by which time there can be a tapering off in the program.

Once irrigation of fine turf commences, the curator must always be alert to the first sign of any loss of vigour. With summer's approach the greens turf is usually in a consistently moist, firm condition, and retaining this state could virtually mean six months of intensive care.

Accurate assessment of the day-by-day moisture requirements of particular areas of turf is most essential, as it is in this climate that a thin line only divides the excessive application of water from the inadequate. As the days lengthen and sunshine becomes more intense, moisture loss must be corrected in the appropriate areas and at the right time to prevent stress developing in the form of wilt or dry patches. However, achieving complete recovery from wilt is reasonably simple compared with the problems associated with over-irrigation of turf.

Several scientific instruments have become available for the purpose of assessing the moisture content of turf on a daily basis. However, mainly because of the undulating formation of putting greens, the most reliable method of evaluating the situation would be close inspection of each green during the summer months. The result would without doubt contribute greatly towards sustaining healthy swards through to the end of the season. As this time approaches, and the hours of sunshine decrease, the periods of watering should be adjusted accordingly.

Close scrutiny of available weather information, a personal barometer check, and finally the percentage of humidity must be regarded as of vital importance in the day-to-day decisions to apply water to turf, particularly putting greens.

The beneficial effects of rain when compared to artificial watering is always recognised. However, the amount of rain, an evaluation of the turf moisture and the prevailing weather should indicate when the next application is warranted.

Quite often high temperatures are accompanied by humid conditions with little if any wind movement, and it is in such an atmosphere that a decision to irrigate regardless may produce harmful results, as evaporation of moisture from the turf is minimal. In addition, over-watered turf would almost certainly not provide good playing conditions. Alternatively, withholding water altogether, or selective hand-watering of only the dry parts will most likely offset any deterioration on the following day.

The actual method of irrigation, whether it be by automatic, semi-automatic, or manual arrangement, is not important so long as it provides just sufficient moisture to prevent any impairment of the turf occurring on any one day. In this way players will appreciate finding the greens firm, and certainly not in squelchy condition.

Conditions may be noted occasionally where water has been applied copiously without any apparent harm to the turf. This would probably be due to the fact that a coring machine was being used, allowing excess moisture to slowly move downwards, so although the surface may remain soft the grasses manage to survive with few ill-effects. If such a condition becomes evident, watering should cease temporarily, or at least be reduced to permit the turf to return to an optimum state.

Most putting green surfaces are undulating, which to a large extent facilitates surface drainage and eliminates any ponding following irrigation or rainfall. At the same time any prominent contours frequently require special attention during summer conditions, such as direct application to these parts by hand-held syringe in addition to the normal sprinkler coverage. In this way it is possible to avoid any run-off to the lower levels, which never need supplementing anyway.

Pressure through jets or hand syringes must be regulated to form droplets, and not be permitted to discharge as mist, which has no penetrating effect whatever.

Sprinklers of any type must not be allowed to leak from any joint on the fine turf, as the excess will surely find its way to the lower parts of the green and aggravate an already over-watered condition. A sprinkler with a fault of this nature that cannot be rectified should not be used on putting greens.

Rotating sprinklers give the best result when adjusted to revolve at a moderate rate, which allows maximum penetration with a minimum of run-off when taken in conjunction with the time of day of watering sessions.

Differing views are expressed regarding the time for optimum application. After many trials it appears the most suitable hours for irrigating fine turf are from the late evening onwards, with completion by sunrise. The main reasons for this recommendation are that maximum benefit is obtained because evapotranspiration is minimal, interruptions to operation do not occur, and where electricity is used for pumping a lower charge would be applicable. Also the excess water will have time to drain away to leave the turf in a suitable condition for mowing next morning, and the situation for players is favourable at all times.

There are a number of objections to daytime watering including the inconvenience to players caused by operating sprinklers, mowing is unsatisfactory, and the turf is often in an over-moist state during summer heat, which creates an optimum climate for disease to develop, and definitely not the environment in which to produce healthy turf grass for putting greens.

Most sprinklers are designed to cover a circular pattern, and it is always important to choose the type most suitable for particular turf. Nowhere is this more essential than when fine turf is involved.

Some types of sprinklers can be simply controlled to cover any part of the full movement, a useful adjustment if it is necessary to avoid a bunker, or again to give extra water to a selected section of turf. Another sprinkler with a difference, although rotating, is geared to travel along a length of hose, efficiently watering a parallel area by a series of concentric circles as it moves slowly over a selected line. It is small and light, and suitable for putting greens.

It is always important for spinklers to be fixed or placed to include at least three metres of turf beyond the actual perimeters of greens and tees. If a method can be devised whereby the greens and tees are watered in the same operational period, this is always an advantage.

Sprinkler jets, and there are a wide variety, must be selected for their suitability for the type of turf in question. In the case of fine turf areas, sprinklers should discharge fine droplets near the centre graduating to larger drops over the outer diameter, and it is in this outer area that the discharge should be seen to disperse sufficiently to provide uniform coverage.

To check whether a sprinkler does in fact provide uniformity, place receptacles at irregular intervals within the irrigated area, and after a period of operation the amount of water in each should be reasonably similar. Furthermore, as calm conditions usually prevail during the recommended night hours, testing then will give a more equitable evaluation of a sprinkler.

There are two instances when uniform coverage fails to be retained in operation. Firstly, under windy conditions the normal pattern is distorted, and secondly, sprinklers that have a circular application must naturally overlap to avoid leaving acute segments unwatered. Nonetheless, uniformity of cover must be regarded as an essential basic feature in sprinkler design.

A travelling type of sprinkler, although largely superseded by modern methods, is still in use to some extent to-day. It was a boon at its time of development for watering fairways when there were so many new courses being constructed. It is capable of covering a large area from one setting as it travels along a hose up to a length of 152m, which is rolled on to a reel as it operates.

Golf courses situated in different localities and constructed by various methods on a great variety of soils vary accordingly in their water requirements. The maximum need of greens turf under mid-summer conditions in a particular region may be adequately met with four applications weekly, whereas in another situation this may be quite insufficient.

It is always desirable, even where a high soil porosity exists, to allow the turf a respite of at least one period each week from sprinkler watering. Most turf grass problems originate during the times of irrigation, mainly because water has not drained away sufficiently or been absorbed into the soil before another application. Should this be repeated several times without any attempt being made to reduce the quantity, the turf will quickly deteriorate, and require aeration immediately as a first step towards a return to healthy growth.

Aeration of turf is usually performed with hollow-time machines, a process which removes small cylinders of turf along the line of travel. Earlier types of aerators were pulled by hand and were fitted with rows of solid steel tapered tines, which did not produce any noticeable benefit. However, the present-day hollow-tine aerators have been developed to a point where most golf clubs have their own machines, and the work is, in many instances, carried out several times a year on a regular basis.

Irrespective of the reasons, hollow-tining of fine turf should be confined to once-a-year operations as too frequent use of the machine will disrupt the putting surfaces, and repetition will do little to alleviate any turf problem as the holes remain viable for a considerable time.

If after tining a putting green to improve surface drainage there is no apparent benefit but the problem is added to by excess water now being retained for some time in the holes, the best course of action, although a major operation, would be to lift the turf, amend the top 75mm of soil to provide better porosity, and relay the turf to a conformation with adequate surface off-flow.

When an aerating machine is used specifically to overcome summer dry patch in fine turf, the maximum benefit from irrigation to the root area will be achieved by using a small-diameter tine with the depth set at 50mm.

Another type of machine with a different approach, but with a similar result to that provided by the coring principle, consists of an arrangement of rotating twist drills, which drill holes and remove soil as the machine progresses. This method has an advantage over the other type of machine, particularly when hard soil is involved. Also, the holes are not so noticeable because pieces of turf are not removed as such, and therefore, less disruption is caused to a fine turf surface.

It is possible to obtain a vast improvement in the condition of soft over-watered turf following aeration by top-dressing the affected area with finely ground charcoal, and scraping it over in the usual manner. Far from being an inert material, charcoal particles used in this way are able to absorb moisture, which immediately makes the turf firmer, and produces a dark green, healthy growth. Unfortunately however, present-day availability and cost of this material could be deciding factors in its use, other than over small sections of turf.

In certain cases coarse sand or fine gravel is spread over turf that is soft and spongy, and then smoothed off as with top-dressing, working it into the holes in the process. This is intended to facilitate surface drainage and thereby firm the turf. Turf treated in this manner requires some time to recover and return to a true putting surface, mainly because the grasses have to grow through the layer of sterile sand, a disadvantage which must be taken into account before adopting the procedure.

The desirable features for putting green turf, as outlined elsewhere, are firmness, with a smooth and fine-textured surface, but it must also incorporate another quality. The term 'turf', as applied in this case, could perhaps more correctly be described as sod embodying a mass of grass roots, which may if necessary be pared away from the soil to a given thickness and still retain its stability. There have, however, been instances noted where the maintenance program includes frequent coring, and such a type of sod does not evolve, or becomes practially non-existent, and usually there is a consequent loss of essential firmness. Similarly, on soils with a less permeable nature, the coring program should be appraised with the view of extending the periods between the operations whenever possible to ensure coring is kept to a minimum.

Where golf courses are situated on high porosity sandy soils coring of the fine turf areas should not be necessary, providing an efficient cultural policy operates, and surface drainage is wholly effective. Furthermore, the operation should not be considered with the idea that subsequent applications of pest control chemicals or fertilisers will be more effective. In fact, if large proportions of such materials infiltrate too deeply, with excessive amounts collecting in the holes, this will cause uneven distribution.

In recent years sophisticated automatic turf irrigation systems have been developed, and installed on many golf courses. Although installation costs are high this is largely offset by savings in actual hours of labour when compared with any previous manual methods of watering. Obviously an adequate water supply is essential for efficiency, and to ensure that the maximum benefit may be derived from such a high capital outlay.

Although these systems operate successfully with a minimum of supervision during the working periods, regular maintenance is necessary, and the type of jets for a particular situation must be carefully determined as with any other method.

Because the automatic method of watering is so much less arduous than manual procedures, those responsible must be alert to the possibility of excess irrigation, especially where fine turf in concerned.

The water requirements of tees and fairways are of a far less exacting nature because the turf in each case is composed of hardier grasses that may be mown less frequently, and at a raised level, thus permitting a much less intensive program of maintenance compared to fine turf. During the summer months, golf course curators try to retain the greens and tees in first class condition. However, usually because of a limited water supply, many are forced to allow the fairways to exist as they may with rainfall only.

When an adequate supply is available, fairway turf is usually irrigated during the summer. However, where the basic grass is *Cynodon dactylon* — couch grass — and it is the intention to fully propagate this grass, caution must be exercised to limit distribution to avoid a constantly over-moist condition. For couch grass to thrive, it requires a well-drained soil with water supplied at intervals to provide conditions that verge on dryness on the one hand, to no more than a moderate degree of moisture on the other. If couch grass vigour is suppressed under peristently created wet conditions, this usually promotes a good cover of annual grasses, and a type of turf often without the firm and durable qualities common to couch grass turf.

Golf clubs with an abundant water supply at hand, and irrespective of the type of soil, often have a policy to produce lush fairways during the summer, and to a somewhat lesser extent, throughout the rest of the year. Therefore they are not overly concerned with couch grass being the basic grass so much as always having well-grassed fairways composed of a variety of grasses. Should soil conditions be unfavourable for growing couch such a plan would undoubtedly provide a desirable option.

Under extremely droughty conditions, fairways that are predominately couch grass will become sparse and thin on the surface, but will quickly revive to a state of vigorous growth when suitable weather returns. This suggests, as has often been proved, that this grass with its vigorous underground rhizomes will survive such conditions as well as thrive with a modicum of water in more moderate circumstances.

---

*Sprinklers may be chosen for their exactness of distribution, however, the wisdom that is vital to healthy turf usually proves to be the timing of each period.*

---

The 5th hole of Royal Melbourne West Course in a natural setting.

Wild native grasses, when allowed to flower, such as this Stipa species, add great interest to the course in spring.

# 14

## Drought conditions and turf survival

Turf managers, particularly where fine turf grass is concerned, should have a pre-conceived plan that may be implemented as soon as possible to meet the emergency of drought and stringent water restrictions. Prolonged dryness occurring in a normally temperate district should be regarded as an indication that unusual measures may become necessary to save valuable turf from serious deterioration.

Drought gradually becomes specific as normal seasonal rainfall fails to materialise, finally resulting in flow reductions in streams above and below ground, and requiring the imposition of severe restrictions to ensure supplies for essential purposes.

In such a situation, one can expect the restraint on the use of water for any industry with a low priority, such as turf maintenance, to become quite harsh as the drought worsens. As the position deteriorates, top priority must be given to the fine turf of the putting greens.

Many golf clubs have dependable internal schemes which in some cases permit extensive watering direct from bores or storages. Other clubs, through necessity, must rely wholly or partially on public supply.

During such times, when fine turf is under severe stress, the principal objective must be to keep the grasses alive, which will probably involve some loss of quality. This, however, may be restored with little difficulty upon the return of more favourable weather.

Following introduction of water restrictions, fine turf must be supported by any means which will fully conserve the water applied. For instance, the raising of the mowing height and less frequent mowing are fundamental and essential procedures which will contribute greatly towards reducing evaporation.

In addition, in such an extreme situation and as an ultimate effort to prevent moisture loss, a light application of a mulch such as malt-house waste — malt combings — over the turf usually proves beneficial. It is also a slow-acting mild fertiliser, is gradually absorbed into the turf and does not affect putting. Turf thus treated has a better chance of survival over a longer period with a minimum of water. The situation can be enhanced by the careful use of hand syringes to avoid wastage through run-off.

Further, when fine turf is under stress through dryness, any form of mechanical treatment such as coring should not be attempted because of a tendency for moisture to dissipate more readily, thereby aggravating rather than benefiting the situation.

There may be a temptation on the part of management, because of the difficulties being experienced in maintaining growth during a prolonged dry period, to allow the turf to fail on the assumption that it would be more economical for it to be re-established from seed at a later date. Any suggestion of this nature would be contrary to most curators' principles, and would no doubt be discarded in favour of making an all-out effort to ensure that the turf survived.

Either way, high costs would be involved but should the latter option be adopted there would be far less disruption to the course, and greater cause for gratification on the part of the curator.

---

*Severe water shortages can prove catastrophic to fine turf grass; past experience must be drawn upon to prevent any turf loss.*

---

# 15

## Turf-laying procedures

Turf culture must include the necessary expertise to lay turf. This ability may be required to rectify any deterioration as quickly as possible in greens and/or tees. Even fairway renovation may be indicated in certain areas.

By applying the method of lifting and relaying, turf can be re-established precisely, and more promptly, than by other means.

Turf surfaces often have imperfections that may have developed over the years, or even originated during construction. Whatever the cause, an efficient procedure causing a minimum of inconvenience to players is always appreciated.

For a project of this nature to be successful, it is essential that the value of the replacement turf be assessed against the quality of the existing turf, particularly when a section only of a putting green is involved.

Should it become necessary to make a major correction involving an entire putting green where the original grasses have largely been overtaken by undesirable species, and it is intended to relay the same turf, while the alteration to the surface will no doubt prove successful no improvement in the botanical composition of the turf can be expected as a result of the operation.

It is essential to maintain a nursery of good quality turf of a suitable area, and to re-establish it as turf is removed. There are excellent sod-cutting machines available that permit the turf to be cut accurately and neatly, which in itself contributes greatly towards executing this type of work effectively and economically.

The labour costs involved in the case of fine turf, such as a putting green, may be assessed on a rate of 30–45 minutes per square metre of turf. A similar figure could be reasonably correct for lifting and relaying such turf as tees, tennis courts, or other level areas.

Providing careful preparations are made prior to beginning the work there is every possibility the time will be kept to a minimum. However, there are occasions during the relaying when careful attention to the moulding of an undulating feature of a putting green will require extra time.

Over a period of perhaps 25 years of regular top-dressing with soil, putting green surface irregularities develop, plus a significant amount of root-mat forming beneath the surface. This material will accumulate to a stage where it will create

71

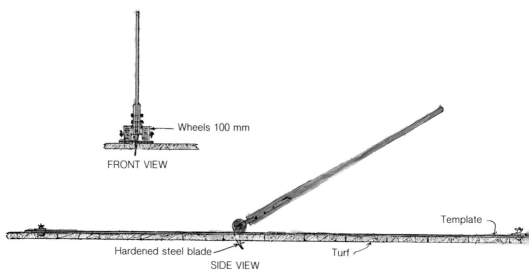

Wheels 100 mm

FRONT VIEW

Template

Hardened steel blade    Turf
SIDE VIEW
Turf cutting tool to be used in conjunction with the template

Turf cutting equipment.

sponginess and retain excessive moisture near the surface, and for these reasons it must be removed. Despite these conditions, however, the grass usually remains quite healthy on the surface, a fact which will prove beneficial to the turf during and after relaying, the object of the exercise being to regain a firm, true putting surface that will be possible to sustain for many years.

When a date to proceed has been decided upon, a temporary green must be prepared a short distance away, so that players will not impede the work. A reasonable surface only need be provided on the fairway, as play should return to the relaid green within a month.

There are, however, several important considerations when planning an operation of this kind. Firstly, if there is any special event scheduled during the following two months, it would not be good policy to proceed. Furthermore, for the most satisfactory results, the cooler months are favoured as moisture loss is minimal while the turf is stacked, the moist turf cuts truly, and lays most readily, and the relaid turf has time to re-establish on the surface as well as in the root area before the warm days of summer arrive. Also, at this time of the year the growth rate throughout the course is much slower, allowing deferral of some of the usual maintenance tasks for a few days without detriment so that as full a complement as possible be employed on the project. Thus the work can be organised so that the various operations follow one another without delays, and the players use the temporary green for a minimum period only.

If reasonable growth is not apparent in the area to be treated, fertiliser should be applied several days before operations are due to begin.

Two wooden straight-edges, 5.5 and 4.5 m long respectively, 100 wooden pegs 30cm long by 25mm square, a good quality builders' line, together with a dumpy level, and boning rods must all be in readiness.

Any particular features considered desirable to retain in the same position and at the same height on a putting green must be noted and fixed by measurement and level to pegs sited well clear of the work, and to be referred to at the appropriate time. As an extra precaution, a plan of the green should be drawn to indicate other desirable features which may be inadvertently altered during operations.

Pegs fixed at 3m intervals and 2m from the normal perimeter of the green before cutting the turf will provide a clear guide later to exactly where the outline of the green should be.

By observing these recommendations, it is then possible to return contours and other significant points to their original positions in the design. On the other hand, if some change is contemplated these indications may still be a useful reference.

At this stage, the cutting of the turf may proceed, with the machine adjusted to cut 28mm thickness, and in a straight line through the longest axis of the area, continuing until the whole is completed. The operator must extend each cut to approximately one metre beyond the green perimeter to permit a square end to be cut by hand just clear of the green, thereby leaving the tapering end of turf in place in each case.

A method of mechanical cross-cutting must be devised to dissect the turf into 1.8 m lengths. A bunker edging machine is adaptable for this purpose, the precise measurement being indicated to the operator by a line stretched across the turf at right angles.

The turf may then be firmly rolled and carried to form stacks at several points around the site. Any undesirable grass, such as couch, detected in the turf should be discarded and alternative sods obtained from another source to complete the work.

Following the removal of the turf, if evidence of a definite thickness of root mat or some other deleterious material remaining is apparent, the sod-cutter can often be used in a similar manner as before to facilitate its removal. When disposal of the root mat is complete, the area must be rotary hoed to a fine tilth and fresh soil spread over the surface to replace, in part at least, the material discarded, and the whole consolidated to a reasonable degree of firmness. Pegs are then fixed at 3m spacings over the area, and soil is added where required to maintain an overall level with the tops of the pegs as they represent the underside of the turf.

Special attention is essential when establishing the pegs, particularly those which will indicate points of fall for surface drainage, and other undulating features inclusive to the conformation.

Each person employed laying turf must be supplied with a wooden hand-mallet to use for firming the turf into position, and a straight-edge 2.4 m long, both edges accurate and reduced at each end by the width and thickness of the sods which will permit its use as a screed off the guide-lines, and thus prepare the bed for each piece of turf.

With the aid of the long straight-edges and the builders' line, guide-lines of turf exactly 1.8 m apart are now carefully laid to levels denoted by the pegs, constantly checking with adjacent pegs to ensure that the resultant conformation will accord with the planned undulations. The re-laying of the turf may proceed as soon as two guide-lines have been established.

The short straight-edges can now be used by those laying the turf and will reach across two guide-lines, enabling each piece of turf to be laid at right angles, and tamped precisely and firmly into position.

As the guide-lines are completed, more people should be employed to relay the turf, and as a further facility, one should be engaged to carry the sods to those laying the turf, to avoid any delay at this point.

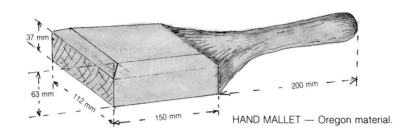

37 mm
63 mm
112 mm
150 mm
200 mm

HAND MALLET — Oregon material.

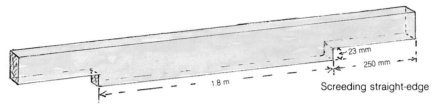

23 mm
250 mm
1.8 m

Screeding straight-edge

Material: 100 mm × 22 mm kd hardwood.

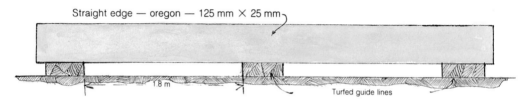

Straight edge — oregon — 125 mm × 25 mm

1.8 m

Turfed guide lines

One plain straight-edge 150 × 25 mm, long enough to reach over
three guide lines of turf.

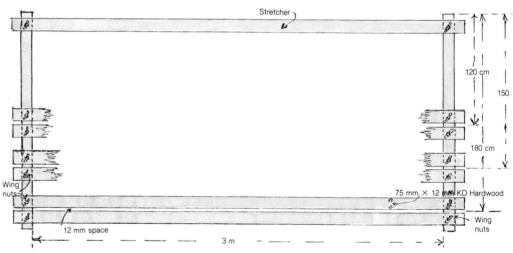

Stretcher

120 cm
150
180 cm

Wing
nuts

75 mm × 12 mm KD Hardwood

Wing
nuts

12 mm space

3 m

A template for cross cutting small areas of turf. The guide
rails may be adjusted to cut turf to lengths of 120, 150, and
180 cm.

Essential items of equipment for turf laying.

Sufficient top-dressing should be prepared beforehand and applied when the work is completed.

Depending upon how skilfully the work is executed, a putting green treated in this way may be re-opened for play in approximately ten days after completion.

This method of laying turf must necessarily form a visible pattern throughout the surface. However, this appearance soon becomes less obvious and will disappear after several weeks.

Although at first the finished surface is somewhat variable for putting, the players generally prefer to return to the green proper rather than continue with the temporary green for an extended period.

It is advisable to move the hole more frequently than usual, and it should be positioned towards the walk-off side of the green for several weeks, or until the turf begins to re-establish.

The various associated problems that give rise to turf-laying procedures for putting green turf, including sponginess, excessive moisture retention, and undulations that have become too abrupt (a situation which usually develops gradually over many years of maintenance) are difficulties that can be solved by the methods described, and as a result the putting surfaces should be firm and healthy, with a fine texture. Smaller isolated patches of inferior turf may also be replaced by the same methods.

If the replacement turf is not of equal quality, it is often more practical to take turf from the side of the green to repair sections in the centre, using the inferior turf where it would not be so noticeable. Should it be impractical to use the sod-cutter in such cases, the waste should be removed by hand-work, and if necessary a screeding straight-edge made to suit the area.

Next in importance to the putting greens is the turf of the teeing areas. The formation of tees should basically be a flat plane, but after some years the surfaces become uneven for a variety of reasons, not the least of which is the over-filling of divots with soil. By employing the method as described for putting greens, this situation can be rectified without difficulty.

However, where flat surfaces are concerned, such as tees, lines of pegs are fixed at 2.1 m spacings which will allow the guide-lines of turf to be laid centrally over the pegs, leaving a space of 1.8 m between for the lengths of turf to be laid at right angles, as detailed for putting greens.

The following provides details of a satisfactory and economical method of laying fairway turf where large areas are involved. The advantage of using sods for such a project on an established course is that play may continue with little delay.

Turf of good quality, capable of being handled without disintegrating, is a requisite for success. When planning such an operation, and to further increase the quality, the turf must receive special fertiliser treatment well in advance of the date arranged to commence the work.

There could be several reasons for work of this nature to be undertaken, such as a redesign of a hole, or a fairway extension. With the former case the existing turf could, in all probability, be removed and relaid in the new design. The area would require to be rotary hoed and harrowed, and raked over by hand to form a bed for the sods, which should be cut into lengths of 1.2 m by 32mm thickness. These pieces are then lifted, not rolled, and placed upon a tray body of a suitable vehicle and taken to the site, and in one operation they can be lifted off singly, and placed together on the prepared soil.

Generally with turf work in a situation of this nature, level pegs are not required, unless there are indications of a drainage difficulty calling for special attention with the surface formation.

Upon completion of the turf-laying, a tractor-drawn roller can prove useful in smoothing over any imperfections. Finally an application of fertiliser is usually advisable.

*Turf laying is an art in which expertise is achieved with practice.*

# 16

## The home lawn

Wherever grass is grown to form turf, quality is as variable as the uses for which it is intended, and unfortunately, for a number of reasons most home lawns may be described as being mediocre.

There appears to be general agreement that a distinctive lawn complements both the house and garden in any location. However, achievement of a lawn of comparable quality to the home and other parts of the garden remains elusive, even after much effort and expense have been incurred.

The basic requirements for a good lawn are a surface that can be mown uniformly and selected grasses free from unwanted plants, with the facility to maintain neatly trimmed edges.

The standard of turf aimed for many be something less than a professionally achieved putting green quality, which is obtained largely by low level and frequent mowings, and certainly not expected in the home or institutional situation. In most cases mowing once a week at a height of 12.5mm would be satisfactory; by comparison putting greens are maintained at about 3.2–6.4mm mowing height.

A plan of the area can often prove helpful and economical if drawn up in the initial stage, showing pathways, mower strips, drainage and water pipe-lines, with positions of trees, and shrubs, etc.

The original conformation of the land can often present problems during preparations, as well as in maintenance of the lawn. Therefore, where there is an excessive slope involved, it may be more practical in the long term to terrace the area to avoid the problems usually associated with maintaining turf on a grade that is too abrupt. Sloping or undulating lawns are always attractive, but features of this nature must be very gradual in concept to minimise difficulties with mowing and watering.

To commence operations, all contractors' and builders' waste such as off-cuts, clay and sub-soil must be carefully removed from the lawn site, or buried deeply, retaining the top-soil in its proper place. Similarly, when any excavation has taken place within the lawn area, the top soil must be set aside and returned later to conform to the final levels.

When a garden contractor is engaged to carry out the work, whether the job is large or small, it is important to have a clear understanding of the methods and materials intended for use. It is also advisable for a short period of after-germination service to be included in the contract. However, the information in this chapter is mainly directed to those home-owners who, once they are aware of the various sequential operations, would derive much satisfaction from doing work of this nature themselves.

Identification and advice should be sought regarding any plants growing naturally on the site, and the best method for their eradication. If any coarse perennial grasses such as couch, kikuyu or water couch, which are widely distributed throughout Victoria, are found growing in an area where it is intended to establish a fine lawn, they must be eradicated. Because of their physical characteristics these three grasses are readily spread by any form of cultivation, which will also increase their vigour, adding to the difficulty of eradication.

As all chemicals available for controlling grasses of this nature are costly, the product chosen for the purpose must be carefully evaluated, chiefly from the point of view of obtaining a positive result. Encroaching roots of nearby selected trees and shrubs are usually a cause for concern when using any toxic material for weed control on an overall basis. On the other hand, if isolated patches only are involved any adverse reaction to plants would be unlikely.

As the grasses mentioned are inactive during the winter months, it is very difficult to quantify the extent of the problem at this time, whereas, over the spring and summer they can be easily estimated and identified.

When there is only a minor infestation apparent, rather than become involved with chemicals, it may be more practical to dig it out by hand work before building operations commence and thus avoid pieces of roots being scattered about the site.

In the case of an established lawn, any isolated patches of unsuitable grassess should be carefully and totally removed when first noticed and the areas resown, or alternatively the patches may be planted with small pieces of grass taken at random from the lawn.

There are a number of total grass killers available, all requiring repetitive treatment to control regrowths, and finally a period of several weeks must elapse before seeding can proceed.

Where there is a high rate of infestation it is preferable to first treat the area as recommended, leave for a week for the material to take effect, then follow up with shallow rotary hoeing once, to encourage regrowths, spraying again when this occurs, and finally hoeing the soil to a fine tilth to a depth of 10cm.

This procedure would apply to treatment with *Dalapon–2, 2–DPA* (Dowpon) (2, 2-dichloropropionic acid), an effective herbicide that has been in use for a number of years.

A more recent formulation recommended as a total herbicide and marketed under the trade name *Roundup* (the active constituent being Glyphosate 36%) has the advantage of being systemic. It does not contaminate the soil, which allows seeding to proceed after a short period of standing to allow the chemical to move through the plants.

All chemicals recommended for weed control are made available for general use with the proviso that certain basic precautions detailed on the label are observed in storage and handling.

As new weedicides are constantly being developed, and often prove to be more efficient than those previously recommended, it is important to seek advice regarding a specific problem before purchasing a product.

For successful results with any material for the control of perennial grasses it is necessary to make the application at a time of vigorous growth and when the soil is moist. Selected plants in close proximity to the work must be protected with polythene sheeting against spray drift, followed by hosing the foliage as an extra precaution when the spraying is completed.

Any weed seeds which germinate during the last standing-time period, such as capeweed or dandelion, must be removed by hand-hoeing or spot-spraying with *Roundup* in preference to the use of the total herbicide again, which could further delay sowing of the seed. Summer grass seedlings (*Digitaria sanguinalis*) often germinate profusely in new work and must be controlled by hand-hoeing, or sprayed with *Roundup* at an early stage of growth before sowing.

With the rotary hoeing completed, the surface should then be formed to approximate the final levels designated by paths and garden-bed edging. Should any major alteration to the surface be necessary to achieve this, the top-soil must be put aside, sufficient sub-soil removed to meet the case and the top-soil replaced.

At this stage of the preparations, the installation of agricultural piping is usually a good investment for the future health of the lawn and garden.

When such a scheme is carefully laid, to discharge into an external drain as described in chapter 6, it will prove most effective in disposing of sub-surface water, which may at times be aggravated by flow from adjoining properties. If such an occurrence is a probability the piping should be laid to intercept any water from this source.

If an underground sprinkler system is contemplated for the lawn, it should also be carefully installed at this stage, bearing in mind the final levels of the surface.

Should the existing soil be considered unsuitable for preparing the seed bed, it would be advisable to obtain selected clean sandy soil for the purpose. This would need to be 25mm thick over the surface.

After consolidating the soil as a whole to a moderately firm condition by rolling or trampling, pegs 25mm square are then firmly fixed at 1.8 m intervals corresponding to the levels of the paths and edgings. From these points lines of pegs are then located across the area, the tops defining the conformation of the finished surface.

Effective surface drainage is important to obviate ponding occurring at any point in the future, a possibility that can be avoided if the pegs are fixed with a minimum fall of 25mm in 3m.

Equipment required to establish the levels as described in a small area would include a 3 m–long wooden straight-edge, spirit level, three boning rods, a builders' line, shovel, rake, and a wheelbarrow.

Although basically similar preparations are necessary for larger areas, the use of machinery that is not too large or heavy for performing most of the operations involved is both practical and economical.

Moving the straight-edge over the tops of the established pegs in each section, and raking carefully to accord with the lines thus indicated, will enable the final shaping of the surface of small areas to be achieved.

Soil sterilisation with methyl bromide gas has become a common pre-sowing practice wherever quality turf is envisaged, and is recommended when its use is practical. This gas will destroy all insect and plant life in the soil, including weed seeds, after being sealed under polythene sheeting for three days, with a further two days following the removal of the sheeting to allow the gas to dissipate into the atmosphere, when the fertiliser may be applied, raked over and watered and two days later sowing of the seed may proceed.

This method also permits the surface formation to be completed before the gas is applied. Following vaporisation the recommendations apply as outlined in chapter 8.

Because special knowledge and handling equipment are necessary, a contractor must be engaged to carry out this method of sterilisation. The initial cost of using methyl bromide on small areas can be high. However, as it provides such efficient and long-term control with a minimum delay before sowing, the process tends to become attractive in many situations.

At this stage of the preparations, and before seed-sowing begins, a soil test is advisable. This is obtained by submitting soil samples, taken from points 4m apart throughout the area, to a competent authority. If lime is indicated it must be applied immediately.

Several days after liming, should this be necessary, the next step is to procure a complete fertiliser mixture, 2-2-2, and apply at 28g per 1 sq m together with 5g of organic waste such as rice hulls or peat moss, the total mix then being distributed evenly over the area, and raked and watered into the soil; the organic material will gradually decompose with a beneficial effect to the surface soil.

In southern Victoria the most suitable time for sowing turf grass seed is the early autumn, a time when the soil still retains a degree of warmth to assist germination and forward growth. Should this time be impractical, the alternative would be early October.

Seed of several Agrostis species suitable for the establishment of good quality lawns are available, and include *Agrostis palustris* (creeping bent), *Agrostis tenuis* (brown top or highland bent) and penncross, a hybrid bent. Of these *Agrostis tenuis* forms durable turf, fine in texture and has good colour. It will establish well with normal maintenance in a wide variety of conditions, and can be expected to provide a satisfactory lawn for many years. The turf quality may be enhanced with the addition of chewings fescue, a very fine-leafed grass.

Commercial turf growing has now developed to the point where it is a means of achieving instant lawn. This appears an acceptable proposition in many cases, irrespective of whether the areas are large or small. The initial outlay is more than compensated for by the obvious benefits of having a mature grass cover in a matter of a few days.

The turves must be carefully and firmly laid on a base prepared to predetermined levels as described in the foregoing, excepting that allowance must be made for the turf to be laid in line with the paths and edging.

Because this type of turf is usually supplied thinly cut, it is just as important as with seeding preparations to ensure that perennial grasses and other weed plants are eradicated prior to turfing.

Turfing in this manner may be undertaken over most of the year, the exception being from December through February. However, because the turf is supplied with very little soil, it is important for careful maintenance to be sustained with the object of encouraging new root development. Chapter 15 provides all the necessary directions should this method be adopted.

The vegetative procedure of propagating turf is outlined in chapter 9 and may be successfully employed in the home garden situation if desired. Procuring supplies for this form of planting is usually a problem as commercial availability is uncertain, more reliance being placed on procuring sufficient stock for the project from a private source. Alternatively a small area, 3m square, could be developed from seed beforehand for later planting of the main area.

The most suitable grass for the purpose is *Agrostis palustris* (creeping bent) which may be reduced to small pieces for planting, each with several growing points. The advantage of this method is that the planted pieces do not require such close and careful attention as is required for seedlings, though watering and fertilising are vital as a means of producing a quick cover. Furthermore, where any planned slopes may be likely to create difficulties with seed germination, or if there is any possibility of the seedlings being dislodged by storm water, vegetative planting will assist greatly in stabilising the surface.

On a number of occasions in the past this method was used to establish putting greens and other fine turf areas, and also provided the means of developing a particular variety of grass that was believed to possess desirable characteristics.

Again, preparation of the soil is most important and must be carefully formed to the correct levels. To commence the planting of the stock it is necessary to make several straight and shallow furrows through the area with a light cultivator or hand plough, 10cm apart, into which small pieces of the grass are firmly planted about 15cm apart, the furrows then being carefully filled and made even, leaving a little of each piece of grass protruding. Working from planks, it is more practical to complete three or four furrows at a time.

The grass should make excellent progress if planted out in the spring, though autumn or winter plantings will also prove satisfactory. At a later stage careful mowing to remove any upright growth only will force the development of new stolons over the surface.

After the grass has made good coverage of the surface, rolling in the direction of the furrows followed by a light top-dressing of soil will be necessary to overcome any unevenness created by the rows of grass plants.

The recommendations so far have generally outlined steps to be taken when establishing a good lawn, which is usually accepted as being most appropriate at the front of the house. However, at the rear of the property a neat appearance is equally desirable, but the turf, because of the usual family activities, must be composed of more durable grasses.

Soil preparations for the back lawn are essentially the same with the exception that couch grass in this instance is acceptable. A seed mixture consisting of *Cynodon dactylon* (couch grass) 12g + *Poa pretensis* (kentucky blue) 12g + *Agrostis tenuis* (brown top) 6 g, each at per sq m, will provide a turf with suitable qualities.

The couch and kentucky blue have vigorous underground rhizomes, each complementing the other in the formation of hard-wearing turf. Though the couch grass has a dormant period during the cold months, the other two grasses retain growth and colour throughout the year.

Vegetative planting of the couch may be considered, providing sufficient stock is available, and should be undertaken in the spring. Providing it receives adequate water, fertilisers and regular mowing during the first year of growth, cover of the area should be largely complete by the end of this time. The kentucky blue and brown top may then be sown over the couch in the autumn, and lightly covered with sandy soil as top-dressing.

Whenever garden beds are to adjoin the lawn, it is advisable to form the concrete mower-edging deeper than usual as a barrier against the grass rhizomes becoming a nuisance in the garden soil.

A person who has undertaken the trouble and expense of establishing a good lawn should then exercise care when selecting trees and shrubs for planting in the vicinity of the turf, keeping in mind the fact that the roots will spread out in search of the nutrients and water applied to turf. Also, excessive shading can influence future turf problems usually associated with the growth of mosses and algae.

Part Three

# Special problems in turf maintenance

Anyone involved with golf course turf in a supervisory capacity is always gratified when all the greens are unblemished, and the rest of the turf is in a similar state. Although there is always a genuine concern to achieve this, there are as many problems associated with the production and maintenance of turf as there are putting greens. So it is reasonable to assume that some form of debility may occur at any time, which in serious cases may entail reseeding or returfing.

To adopt either of these methods may provide a simple and effective recovery. If, however, it is possible and time permits, healthy growth may be promoted by some less obvious means. It is often surprising to observe the strong recuperative power of grasses that have been under severe stress.

Time should be taken to study any gradual reaction to the correction of a problem, such as when patches of turf appear dead, but following appropriate treatment healthy growth reappears. Valuable experience for the future can be gained in this way.

Prevention of diseases, and insect and weed infestation is the ideal to be aspired to, and by vigilance and an understanding of the causes of problems relating to turf health, costly and time-consuming treatments can be avoided.

It cannot be denied that turf research must continue, and results will always be of vital interest and assistance to the turf manager.

# 17

## Insect pest control

The depredations of some insect pests in turf, because of their numbers and voracious habits, can be extremely severe in a short time, and are often clearly visible, while other species, because of their minuteness and life cycle differences, are difficult to detect and control.

An error in diagnosis can prove costly, as for example, if a fungicide is applied when an insecticide would have been appropriate, or vice versa. A possible lapse of time before it becomes evident that the application is ineffective allows the problem to become more widespread in the meantime.

Damage resulting from disease mimics that caused by certain insects in fine turf. Although treatment must be prompt, in a confusing situation of this nature a more positive result will be possible if a turf sample is referred to a plant pathologist.

It will not help future diagnoses of similar conditions if fungicide and an insecticide are applied in combination, nor is it advisable to mix chemicals with such diverse functions for application to fine turf.

Weather conditions can produce a distinct unseasonal variation, and may cause a situation conducive to the invasion of a particular insect pest which may not have been noticed in such numbers for many years, if at all.

Fortunately, there are few insect pests that are able to survive present-day recommended insecticides and cause damage to golf course turf on a large scale. Several of these insecticides are known to persist in the soil for some time thus providing control of a number of insects on a long-term basis. This is usually a more practical and economical objective than treating the larvae when they are actively destructive, a stage when they are more difficult to restrain. Furthermore, any damaged turf will require time to recover.

Many insecticides are complex substances that must be handled carefully during preparation and distribution, which must always be consistent with the manufacturer's directions set out on the label.

It is important that applications are made at the appropriate time to allow the insecticide to be absorbed into the soil by rain or irrigation and make contact with the larvae as they hatch, their most vulnerable stage. Also it is the larvae, not the adults, that are usually responsible for damage to turf grasses. For instance, cockchafer larvae and those of the underground grass grubs are species which, when numerous, can seriously impair fairway turf in the autumn, but which may be restrained by applying the recommended insecticide in the spring.

A method frequently adopted for fairway treatment is to request a fertiliser manufacturer to incorporate the requisite amount of insecticide into the dry mixture when placing the order. However, for golf course applications it is preferable to apply insecticides in solution, and under low pressure through a series of in-line jets, and as a separate task.

Although there are a number of cockchafers, there seem to be two species only that destroy turf. These can be recognised by either a red head, *Adoryphorus couloni*, or a black head, *Aphodius tasmaniae*. Their habits are quite different, the latter emerging at night to feed on the grass surface and in so doing raising small casts of soil, and if numerous quickly defoliating the surface with disastrous results where heavy soils are involved. This larvae is relatively easy to control, even when allowed to reach full growth, provided treatment is carried out while grass is still on the surface to retain the insecticide.

The red-head larvae is active below the surface where it feeds on decayed matter. However, it is during this activity in dry autumn conditions particularly that the grass roots are broken off, thus leaving the turf loose for predators in search of the grubs such as the larger birds and some animals, which are capable of disturbing large areas of turf. It is because of this activity in such conditions that the soil often becomes completely dry and powdery, which makes it very difficult for water to permeate, a situation that would not arise, despite the presence of the grubs, if the fairways were irrigated on a regular basis.

As the red-head species remains below the surface, to achieve control the insecticide must be applied in the springtime to be taken by rain to a level of about 35mm below the surface by the time the eggs hatch in the autumn.

Should brown patches appear and birds begin searching by pecking into fine turf of putting greens it is possible the red head larvae are present. In this case the turf should be cut and rolled back, the grubs removed by hand, the turf replaced carefully and watered, and steps taken to avoid a recurrence by applying an insecticide at the time recommended.

Despite the irritation of any disruption this insect can cause it does provide an unusual situation in turf maintenance, in which the pest's predators are responsible for most of the impairment, particularly in the case of fairway turf.

Another major pest of fairway turf, only occasionally found in fine turf, is the underground grass grub, *Oncopera spp*. The adult is a moth and the larvae feed off the surface growth at night in the autumn. The grub is about 30mm long, is a dark grey, and makes a vertical burrow about 15cm deep, lining it with strong web, the web extending for a short distance horizontally just below the surface. The grub feeds from the entrance without completely leaving the burrow; they also collect a number of grass pieces which they store at the bottom of the burrow to be eaten during the day. When this species is numerous with the burrows close together the damage can be quite significant.

A large ground-inhabiting scarab species of black beetle is more often a nuisance rather than a pest as they claw soil to the surface of fairways to form large casts during the autumn when the sub-soil is dry. When they occur in large numbers they create something of a problem for the mowers. The adult and larvae feed on organic matter near the surface and therefore are not actually destructive to turf.

There are two species of insect, namely the Argentine stem weevil and the couch fly larvae or maggot. Both are destructive and because of their minuteness difficult to detect, which often makes identification of the problem uncertain.

Although earthworm activity has a beneficial effect on soils they do cause problems in any type of turf, and accordingly must be controlled. They are usually most active in heavy soils but may occur to a lesser degree in lighter soil types. Where their activities result in numerous casts on the surface of fine turf they then become a nuisance to players and during mowing operations.

It can be confusing when attempting to identify the cause of activity on fairway turf from the casts alone, as both the black-head cockchafer and earthworms can be active in the same area simultaneously. However, the presence of the latter will be indicated by the form of the casts which consist of firm pellets of soil, in contrast to the casts raised by the cockchafer which crumble readily when disturbed.

At times worms will become unusually active in fine turf that has deteriorated in quality, a situation in which it would be advisable to first ascertain and correct the cause of the debility, which will in itself contribute towards controlling the worms. Further, turf in a healthy state can always be expected to withstand to a degree the action of any insect, and thereby respond more readily following treatment.

Nematodes or eelworms have been known to be responsible for significant injury to many species of turf-forming grasses. In the USA where the problem has been recognised and researched for some years, a number of nematode species with various forms of attack were shown to be accountable for a wide range of turf grass, and other plant disorders. They are microscopic, parasitic, and in certain situations can assume great numbers. Their method of feeding is by attaching themselves to the roots which can cause stunting, chlorosis, general debility and malformation of the surface components of the grass plants.

Usually the presence of nematodes coincides with a lack of response to nutrients, insecticides and fungicides applied to fine turf in the course of normal maintenance, although a similar type of turf failure could occur from other causes.

Experience has shown that nematodes are responsible for the development of fairly prevalent deformed growth called 'yellow tuft', which has affected the surface growth of many putting greens in Victoria and elsewhere for a number of years. The treatment for their control consists of spraying the affected turf with a nematacide in the early summer followed by a copious watering. The action of the nematacide is to gasify as it comes into contact with the moist soil. As it is non-selective it will temporarily diminish the population of beneficial organisms in the soil, which gives an indication of the importance of establishing firstly that a nematode problem exists.

To obtain this information, and because they are such minute insects, samples of sod should be referred to a plant pathologist for examination and positive identification, a procedure which is always worthwhile should a confusing turf condition develop and normal treatment fail to produce a satisfactory response. Furthermore turf stress from this source can be discounted if the pathology report on the turf area in question finds the nematode infestation to be of a minor nature only.

A species of native bee sporadically invade and scar fine turf by burrowing into the turf to form nests. As these insects have a beneficial role in nature they should not be treated as a pest. Usually they dislike the climate provided by turf maintenance and soon depart of their own accord.

Similarly, a small species of ant can become a pest at irregular intervals. Because of their habit of nesting in colonies in the soil and leaving casts on the surface of fine turf they must be treated promptly with a suitable insecticide.

Identified in the following table are a number of troublesome insects often found to be responsible for turf damage.

| Scientific names | Common names |
| --- | --- |
| Adoryphorus couloni | red-head cockchafer |
| Annelid worms | earthworms |
| Aphodius tasmaniae | black-head cockchafer |
| Delia urbana | couch tip maggot |
| Hyperodes bonariensis | Argentine stem weevil |
| Nematode spp. (parasitic) | eel worms |
| Oncopera spp. | Underground grass grub, also known as webworm |

## Insect pests affecting trees and shrubs

Most golf clubs cultivate a wide variety of trees and shrubs to form plantations, interspersed with individual specimens. There are a number of pests, many with voracious appetites, which can seriously affect immature trees in particular if they are not promptly controlled.

A wide variety of attractive native species are most suitable for planting on golf courses, but in common with other plants are subject to damage at some time by insects. Therefore it is important that a close examination of young trees is made when there is any noticeable change occurring to the foliage. If leaf-eating insects are responsible they may be readily controlled with a suitable insecticide. However, when the presence of sucking insects is suspected — often they are minute and difficult to detect — it may be necessary to seek advice from a plant pathologist before the damage becomes excessive.

It is often difficult to satisfactorily spray the higher parts of large trees. Nevertheless, where a problem exists an effort should be made to prevent as much defoliation as possible.

The larvae of the saw fly wasp is a fairly common pest which attacks the foliage of young and mature eucalypts alike, coming together to form a cluster during the daytime and moving over the trees to feed at night with dire consequences. Because they are usually in vast numbers they are capable of causing extensive damage if not treated.

The larvae of this insect are active for several weeks before reaching the pupation stage which takes place in the soil, often remaining there for years before the adult saw fly wasp emerges. When the larvae are nearing the end of their active life they descend to the base of the tree to pupate, which provides an opportunity to simply treat large numbers, thus breaking the life cycle.

Outbreaks of lerp insects, which are scale-like in appearance, occur from time to time to attack the foliage of eucalypts. They eat away the substance of the leaves, leaving only the outline and veins intact. This pest can be largely controlled with a systemic insecticide sprayed on as much foliage as possible, avoiding blossom-time, and also by applying the chemical to the soil around the tree where, partly at least, it will be absorbed into the system via the roots to eventually destroy the insects. The soil must be loose to avoid run-off of the insecticide and retain it in the area close to the tree, and be thoroughly watered into the soil.

Systemic insecticides must be handled with a full measure of caution as is recommended for other pesticides, but once they are in the soil or plant foliage they are, in the case of insecticides, far less harmful to natural predators and beneficial insects than some other insecticides.

Thryptomene, a particularly attractive native shrub grown extensively on golf courses, is liable to attack by a species of caterpillar which emerge from cocoons and swarm over the plants, and if not treated with an insecticide will completely defoliate the plants resulting in many failing to survive.

Developing trees and shrubs in particular can be set back significantly by insect attacks, often resulting in lost growth. They do not always recover to produce a natural uniform shape of a species.

Although chemical spraying on a golf course is necessary for insect restraint and other reasons, it must be managed in such a manner that will avoid any risk to neighbours or their property.

It is always important to add the correct quantity of surfactant to insecticidal solution to ensure a thorough coverage of leaf surfaces, especially where smooth leaves are concerned.

For a number of years there have been instances of successful insect control by means of parasites, a method of approach which could become effective over a wider range of insects in the future. However, control at present rests mainly with an application of a suitable insecticide.

# 18

# Weed control

Some weed species are referred to as broad-leafed and are always obvious. However, there are many other weed plants that are less noticeable, but to the experienced eye are just as apparent and objectionable, often being aggressive in habit and progressing at the expense of the selected grasses, particularly in fine turf. Some of the latter colonise to form patches from which the grasses are excluded, and which develop a spongy character.

The most common undesirable grass plants found in fine turf include *Holcus lanatus* (Yorkshire fog) and *Poa annua* (winter grass). Three other coarse grass species commonly found growing in fairway turf and rough areas in varying degrees of infestation are *Paspallum dilatatum*, *Paspallum distichum* (water couch) and *Pennisetum clandestinum* (kikuyu grass).

The wide range of selective hormone herbicides available is frequently being added to as research proceeds. Usually one weedicide can be selected with an active constituent that will control one or several weed species. However, other measures are necessary to eradicate unwanted plants which have grass-like characteristics, such as Yorkshire fog.

To control the coarse, vigorously growing grasses mentioned, it is necessary to resort to more drastic methods which may involve the use of a grass-killer or soil-sterilant.

With so many facilities available for weed restraint there can be no justification for high densities of weeds in turf, a state many species are capable of assuming when there is no policy for control. There have been instances noted from time to time of paspallum and/or kikuyu having become widespread from only a few isolated plants, which could no doubt have been eradicated when they were first noted.

Unfortunately, kikuyu grass is sometimes intentionally introduced into fairways and rough, primarily because of its vigorous growth and low maintenance costs, requiring little if any fertiliser and providing turf which is usually coarse, dense and spongy.

Couch grass is generally preferred as a basic grass for fairways, but, unlike kikuyu grass, which generally excludes other grasses during its dormant period, annual winter grasses will germinate profusely throughout strong couch turf during the dormant period to form excellent fairway turf through to late spring when the couch regrowth begins.

There are a number of broad-leafed species which may be found to a limited extent in most fine turf and which may be readily controlled with selective herbicides. However, caution is advisable when treating small-leafed mat-forming weeds such as pearl wort, *Hydrocotyle spp.* and *Pratia spp.*, which are known to be partially resistant to hormone materials, usually requiring follow-up treatment at the recommended rates to achieve a satisfactory result.

To gain a full understanding of the reaction of a herbicide on unwanted plants in fine turf, it is always desirable to firstly conduct tests on a modified scale.

Prior to the advent of selective herbicides, all available weed control materials were phytotoxic and their use restricted to fairway turf, which could only be undertaken by careful hand-spotting of weeds from pressure supplied by a mechanical pump, and to avoid as far as possible any damage to the grasses in the process, which would in turn limit the area of soil rendered temporarily sterile. This method often resulted in an unsatisfactory percentage of control, was labour-intensive and in many cases considered uneconomical, with the final effect being high densities of broad-leafed weeds on many golf fairways.

The only alternative to spot-spraying, with its resultant dead patches, was to make a total effort to control broad-leafed weeds with hand tools, a formidable task and a method which also left bare patches. However, these would quickly recover. Similarly, this was considered to be the most suitable method for keeping the turf of greens and tees free of weeds, and even to-day, where there are but a few weeds involved, hand-weeding is often preferable to an over-all chemical spraying.

Therefore, when suddenly efficient selective herbicides were introduced, which were so totally different to any previous materials, it was obvious that, to obtain the maximum benefit from such impressive chemicals, a satisfactory method for their over-all distribution on fairways and other large areas of turf had to be evolved because, although the spraying materials were available suitable machinery for application was not. However, this state of affairs did not continue for long, as soon afterwards a number of manufacturers began producing booms with a row of accurate jets for attaching to tractor power take-off shafts. Now with subsequently designed improvements, the current models are very efficient, enabling the spraying of a golf course to be completed in about three days.

To ensure a satisfactory result, it is of the utmost importance for control measures to be taken at the optimum time, for instance if weeds are allowed to mature, ripened seeds will then be dispersed naturally with a consequent mass of seedlings, thus sustaining the population.

Despite the fact that efficient spraying units are in general use, evidence suggests that a percentage of weeds escape, and together with seeds derived from outside sources the species are able to reproduce. The former instance indicates the necessity for care to be exercised by the operator, with each pass of the machine.

When the work is performed in a thorough manner the number of weeds apparent in a succeeding year should be minimal, and in most cases it should be possible to maintain a satisfactory level with two-yearly applications of herbicide. On the other hand, fairway turf with a high weed population initially would undoubtedly require repeat treatments for several years to achieve a satisfactory level.

Although selective weedicides have provided management with the means to restrict weeds in turf, it must virtually remain a recurring exercise to maintain a satisfactory situation throughout the turf of greens, tees, fairways, rough and other out-of-play areas within the boundaries of a golf club.

It is always important to carefully read the label on the container or elsewhere, including the fine print, relevant to the manufacturer's recommendations for handling a material. Some of the hormone formulations are extremely volatile, therefore, for a consistent result weather conditions must be taken into account. Also, the probability of damage accruing to plants or crops in adjacent properties must certainly be taken into consideration, for obvious reasons.

Whenever hormone spraying is carried out close to cultivated plants, even though the weather conditions may be calm, it is advisable to take the precaution of hosing down the nearest plants with clean water immediately, to avoid damage from spray drift.

It may be found in certain districts, despite care in application, that some weed species have a resistance to the generally accepted material used in other localities, and therefore may require trials with other formulations in the range to obtain a satisfactory reaction.

The principle of a weed eradication program must be based on the whole property, including inaccessible areas, which would require use of a one- or two-jet hand-lance fitted to a length of hose under low pressure from the power unit. This method has proved satisfactory for controlling weeds in sections of important turf on the verges of greens, tees and bunkers, where it is often impractical to obtain complete cover during normal wide-boom spraying of the fairways.

Before starting a spraying schedule of the fairways, it is recommended that mowing be omitted on one prior occasion to allow the weeds to be complete, and thus absorb the maximum amount of the weedicide, and for the same reason mowing should not be resumed until several days after completion of the work.

Fertiliser applications improve turf cover, and thereby generally assist in reducing weed populations. However, when weeds are present even to a minor degree, they will grow larger and more vigorously after receiving the benefit of the fertiliser. Therefore it is desirable to implement weed control before fertilising. Furthermore, by following this sequence any scars that may occur on the turf as a result of double application or a malfunction in the unit can then be expected to make a quicker recovery.

In special situations where weeds have to be eradicated from turf that is partially enclosed with cultivated plants, spot-spraying with a low pressure would be far less hazardous to the plants than blanket spraying.

The dilution rate for spotting must be modified from that recommended for boom spraying, which will vary according to the concentrated material selected for the work. If this information is not noted on the container the manufacturer should be consulted. To avoid over- or under-application when spotting, it is advisable to colour the solution with a rhodamine dye, and work between two stretched cords about a metre apart.

The use of herbicides on seedling turf is not recommended because of the risk of damage. In this situation, and depending upon the extent of the problem, hand-weeding can be an effective method of eradication if carried out at an early stage of growth, or spraying may be delayed until the turf becomes more mature.

There are several species of trifolium frequently found in golf course turf, which are broad-leafed and conspicuous and often found growing in dense patches, and therefore must be controlled. Lush clover of this type can often be associated with a heavy application of superphosphate. On the other hand the problem is less likely to occur in turf that receives regular applications of nitrogen, a fact which is obvious in the case of fine turf, where clover is usually confined to a few small scattered plants as a result of frequent applications of nitrogen.

Golf course fairways on a loamy soil that retains a slightly acid reaction pH 6.5 will often produce a natural vigorous growth without the need for regular fertiliser treatment, a condition that can also induce a high degree of clover infestation, which will require repeated applications with a selective clover control spray. The problem seldom becomes significant on fairways which have a more acid soil reaction as a result of a fertiliser program that has included regular applications of nitrogen, plus carefully assessed amounts of superphosphate and potash.

Applications of hormone herbicides during the winter months should be avoided, as quite often at this time when the vigour of the grasses is at a low level these materials can have a depressing affect on the turf. This would not be evident later when the growth is progressive; also the weeds are more susceptible when growing vigorously.

A guiding principle in turf management should always be to use herbicides at the recommended dilution, at a time when the maximum effect may be expected and only when a condition requires to be corrected, the main reason being that, although some hormone materials are known to break down quickly, there are others which have been found to persist in the soil for many months under certain conditions.

If the effect of any chemical is not fully understood by the person responsible, trials should be undertaken or advice sought before proceeding.

A non-selective herbicide has proved very satisfactory for eradicating troublesome grass plants in many situations. It is systemic in its action with the added advantage of not leaving any toxic residue in the soil, and after standing two weeks to allow the plants to fully absorb the chemical, reseeding may proceed. It is marketed under the name of *Roundup*, active constituent Glyphosate. It has proved effective with such perennial weed grasses as paspallum and kikuyu in fairways and rough. However, care must be taken to avoid transference of the toxic material while moist to untreated turf by restricting all traffic on the treated area until it has dried thoroughly. In certain situations individual unwanted plants may be neatly and effectively eliminated by painting them with the solution.

It is imperative that all spraying equipment be thoroughly cleaned before re-use on or near selected plants.

Owing to the wide variation in the use of common names, it is advisable for a turf manager to become conversant with the botanical names of the relevant plants as this knowledge is an advantage in discussions regarding weed control in particular. Instances have been noted, even in turf publications, where local names of plants have been used without botanical names, which does not always assist interested readers to fully understand a particular problem.

The following table includes a number of troublesome weeds often found in turf, and a number of other unwanted plants which are quite common to golf courses. The latter category include proclaimed noxious weeds. For their control advice should be sought from the appropriate government authority.

| Botanical name | Common name |
|---|---|
| *Arctotheca calendula* | cape weed |
| *Erodium spp.* | storksbill |
| *Cerastium vulgatum* | mouse ear chickweed |
| *Gnaphalium spp.* | cudweed |
| *Hydrocotyle spp.* | pennywort |
| *Hyperchoeris radicata* | flatweed |
| *Juncus articulatus* | jointed rush |
| *Juncus bufonius* | toad rush |
| *Mesembryanthemum spp.* | pig face |
| *Plantago coronopus* | carrotweed |
| *Pratia pendunculata* | trailing pratia |
| *Soliva sessilis* | onehunga |
| *Sagina procumbens* | pearlwort |
| *Trifolium spp.* | clover |

In addition to the above there are also a number of troublesome common grass species that intrude into turf and must be removed, particularly when the purity of fine turf is threatened. Because of their growth structure grasses are not affected by hormone weedicides when applied at the manufacturer's recommended rates, and therefore require other methods of control, a number of which are noted in the following table.

## Botanical name

*Cynodon dactylon* (couch grass) If practical remove from fine turf and replace with nursery turf, depending on the degree of infestation, and if this is high, it may be more economical to sterilise the area with methyl bromide and returf, or resow.

*Digitaria sanguinalis* (summer grass) It is not uncommon for numerous seedlings of this species to appear in newly sown turf, and they should be removed with a small sharp-edged tool from the four-leaf stage onwards.

*Holcus lanatus* (Yorkshire fog) Because of its lighter green colour and wide leaf blades it always mars fine turf, and should be replaced with nursery turf.

*Paspallum dilatatum* (paspallum) If plants are scattered hand weeding may be employed, or spot-spray with *Roundup* if numerous.

*Paspallum distichum* (water couch) In fine turf, remove affected turf and replace with suitable nursery sods.

*Pennisetum clandestinum* (kikuyu grass) This grass should be strictly controlled and prevented from establishing itself anywhere on a golf course, particularly in fairway turf, where it would be advisable to use a total grass killer, and after the required standing has elapsed replant with couch grass.

*Poa annua* (winter grass) Refer to chapter 21.

Listed below are some well-known proclaimed noxious weeds often found on golf courses around southern Victoria.

*Chrysanthenoides monilifera* (bone seed plants)
*Lycium ferocissimum* (box thorn)
*Rubus fruticosus* (blackberry)
*Salpichroa origanifolia* (pampas lily of the valley)
*Ulex europaeus* (gorse or furze)

Photography: Roger Gould

4th West, 5th West and 13th West Course greens and bunkering, set amongst dwarf native plants and wild grasses.

Photography: Roger Gould

The turf of tees, fairway and green on holes 6th and 7th West Course.

# 19

## Control of turf diseases

The present-day practice of turf culture is generally far more intensive than was the case during the years up to 1950, and herein may be found the reason why fine turf grass plants are now more likely to be subject to virus attack.

There can be no question that the number of diseases affecting turf has increased, and many of the pathogens are extremely virulent, particularly where putting greens are concerned, the area in which management continues to aspire for perfection under all conditions.

As a result of these problems much information has become available, in many cases through scientific research, in combination with a number of effective control materials for application whenever the health of fine turf in particular is threatened.

Of major importance in this area is the progress made in the USA with hybrid selection, the varieties having the characteristics of the most desirable growth features, and resistance to many disease pathogens. The seeds of these strains are now available in Australia, and will no doubt be of great benefit in the culture of fine turf in the future.

Much of the putting green turf currently produced can be described as being prone to disease whenever the slightest environmental change occurs, and therefore any research that produces benefits in this area must be of inestimable value to all those involved.

It is imperative that the turf manager realises the importance of limiting the application of fertilisers to avoid producing lush growth, particularly at a time when other factors may also be conducive to disease attack.

When a particular example of turf is described as perfect for putting, differences of opinion often arise among players, revolving around whether the surface should be firm and fast, or slow and soft. However, from the practical point of view, there is a general consensus among turf workers that a relationship exists between optimum climatic conditions and the severity and recurrence of turf diseases, and such a relationship applies more to the slow, soft conditions than to firm and closely mown turf.

Diagnosis of a problem may often be confusing. It has been found on a number of occasions, following an examination of turf by a plant pathologist, that two or more disease-producing organisms responsible for damage are present simultaneously in the soil, becoming active only when conditions are favourable, thereby adding to the extent of the injury.

Frequent checking of the turf is important during periods when the weather favours disease attacks, and at the first indication of any problem of this nature, treatment must be applied promptly to prevent it becoming more extensive. Further, a return to healthy growth cannot be expected without correct fungicidal treatment.

Most turf pathogens become active in the grass plants at optimum atmospheric and soil temperatures, and become less active when a definite seasonal change to lower temperatures occurs. For example a situation of this kind can arise in the wake of a late autumn attack in which the disease will appear to subside and not warrant treatment as the cold weather approaches. However, without attention, and although barely noticeable, it will over-winter and become active in the same turf again in early summer, often before the problem would otherwise arise.

Although there are a number of basic environmental conditions in which fungi will cause severe damage to fine turf, fortunately there are also efficient fungicides from which to choose to obtain satisfactory control in almost any situation. However, it is doubtful if there is any one material which can be recommended with confidence for the control of all fungi. Nevertheless it is advisable to select one fungicide that is known to give control over a wide spectrum, and avoid being involved with a number of materials which can often produce confusing results.

The course curator should have an understanding of the constituents of any fungicide intended for use, particularly with regard to any possible adverse residual effect on the soil.

Mercuric chloride (corrosive sublimate) has been used with success for turf disease control extending over many years and it has a broad range of control, in most cases for four or five weeks duration. Also it is often included as a constituent in more recent commercial fungicides. These materials are costly and extremely poisonous to humans, therefore it is essential to use care in handling and with application. Also they are phytotoxic if applied to turf at rates above those recommended.

Phenyl mercuric acetate (PMA) is an organic mercury material which will control a number of turf diseases, in particular dollar spot disease, and fusarium patch. It is available as a liquid concentrate.

To obtain the maximum benefit from fungicides, it is important to adhere to the manufacturers' recommended rates of application, to withhold watering for 24 hours, and avoid applying fungicides during high temperatures as temporary scorching of the turf can often result.

A development in plant disease control has been the introduction of the systemic fungicide benomyl (Benlate) which controls a number of turf grass diseases.

The effectiveness of a fungicide must always be evaluated in association with well-founded maintenance procedures. A contribution to such a judgement can often be made three or four days after the application by examining the diseased patches with a magnifying glass to detect the first sign of young grass shoots growing out of what may appear to be dead turf. Any new shoots that are green and unmarked would indicate regeneration. However, the necessity to apply a follow-up application of fungicide must not be overlooked at this time. On the other hand, should the young growth emerge discoloured, it could indicate continuing fungal activity, and maybe a change of fungicide would be an advantage.

In situations where the turf is affected with a disease and algae are also present, it is recommended that the fungicide *Dithane M 45* (active constituent mancozeb 80%) be applied, which will eliminate the algae and also have a restrictive influence on the fungus.

It is very important to stress any aspect of turf maintenance that will assist in creating an unfavourable environment for disease organisms to attack the turf. It is often apparent that a specific fungal activity has occurred as a result of combined natural and created conditions, therefore any program designed to control the incidence of turf disease must involve cultural practices as well as fungicides.

It is significant that the areas of turf least susceptible to disease are the well-drained, almost dry prominent parts of undulations. It is also clear that turf weakened by the incursion of tree roots and subject to more shade than sunlight, with a climate in which air circulation and turbulence is minimal, particularly at the turf surface, is more vulnerable to fungus attack of an extended nature.

Other maintenance factors to be considered during the susceptible months are the adherence to a minimum use of fertilisers, watering requirements being carefully assessed on a daily basis, and mowing with wire brushes attached, at a height and frequency of cut which will retain a proper and acceptable putting surface.

Daily weather forecasts are usually reliable in regard to temperature and humidity, and it should be possible with this information, plus on the spot experience, to deduce whether water should be applied to the turf normally or on a restricted basis.

Humidity is usually attended by calm weather, a condition when the transpiration rate is considerably reduced, often despite high temperatures, and the moisture content of the turf is therefore critical at such times. This often requires that modified watering, possibly substituting a limited time with hand-held syringes if necessary, replace the usual sprinkler periods.

In direct contrast to this situation is a combination of high temperatures and strong drying winds with low humidity. This denotes a high evapotranspiration process, and therefore the turf is less prone to disease, but again, water requirements are vital and must be more generously assessed to avoid any deterioration of the grasses through dryness.

Common and related summer turf problems are dryness and wilt: the grasses wilt because dryness has occurred in the root area, which, if allowed to continue can result in deterioration of the turf to a point where recovery cannot be expected. However, provided an effort is made to correct dryness as it occurs a complete recovery is possible. On the other hand it is much more difficult, and often impossible, to obtain a favourable response from turf that has degenerated as a result of being constantly subject to excess moisture.

Quite often where a bad drainage condition exists in an area of fine turf the incidence of disease is constant and difficult to control, a situation which can only be rectified by making the drainage effective.

Fine turf can benefit greatly at most times of the year by disturbing the surface during mowing, on a regular basis, with light attachments such as the steel brushes already mentioned, and metal rakes, set in a manner that will not unduly disrupt the surface or interfere with putting, but is nevertheless sufficient to improve the access of sunlight and air to the soil surface between the grass stems.

During favourable conditions, this treatment has proved particularly useful in reducing the severity of fungal diseases by creating a healthier superficial situation, especially on turf wet with dew, which is usually a critical environment for fungal activity. A clear example in dewy conditions is the wispy mycelium of dollar spot disease, indicating that the causal fungus is present — with perhaps other less obvious fungi — and must be arrested, firstly by raking and brushing, followed by an application of fungicide.

The siting of putting greens in tree-sheltered settings always produces delightful effects, and usually any suggestion to remove established trees is resisted. However, cutting back and thinning the lesser growth to improve air circulation would create a site less prone to fungal activity, and generally have an influence on the good health of the turf. The importance of applying a minimum of water in any one period to fine turf in such problem surroundings cannot be over-stressed. The relationship between tree planting and the health of fine turf grass is fully covered in chapter 2.

As there is a definite relationship between the application of fertiliser and the incidence and severity of disease in fine turf, and despite the fact that the use of fertilisers is unavoidable, it is always essential to avoid producing lush over-stimulated grass. This may have a certain appeal, but, apart from providing an environment conducive to fungal diseases, as putting green turf it is not desirable because it is usually spongy with a tendency to hold foot markings. However, it is not to be construed from this that under-nourished turf is immune from attack by fungi, but rather that any such activity is generally less severe and the turf more readily restored to healthy growth.

As an additional precaution on this aspect of turf management, applications of fertilisers during periods of high natural fertility should be restricted, as for instance during the summer and early autumn when warm moist conditions prevail on fine turf areas, and a moderate steady growth is apparent.

The addition of a nitrogenous fertiliser to a fungicide is not recommended but rather a small quantity of fertiliser applied a week later. However, it is significantly beneficial to add a wetting agent, plus 225 grams of iron sulphate per 100 sq m of turf, to any fungicidal solution.

A question that often arises is whether a preventive or curative program of control should be followed. Prevention necessarily involves a high cost for materials and labour to treat eighteen greens once every three or four weeks without an assurance that disease will not occur, at least to some extent. On the other hand, quite often there are a number of greens on a course which for one reason or another remain unaffected and healthy for long periods, thus requiring intermittent treatment which must be implemented immediately a fungus appears, as opposed to a scheduled program of control.

When it is possible to select a fungicide that is known to be fully effective for an identified pathogen, the curative program must be regarded as being preferable, mainly because poisonous substances should be applied only when necessary.

It is advisable to use a fungicide alone and avoid adding other chemicals to a solution intended for fine turf, with the idea of fertilising, or controlling weeds and insects in the same operation.

Past experience of a disease usually permits a satisfactory diagnosis to be made immediately. On the other hand, should identification be necessary, an application of a mercuric fungicide would be prudent while advice is being sought. Knowledge of the scientific name of any causative organism will facilitate the adoption of prompt and correct control measures.

A perplexing diagnostic situation may occasionally arise in turf work because some grass failure has not responded as expected to an application of fungicide, but rather has become progressively worse. In such circumstances it may be wise to apply an insecticide without delay to ensure against any minute insect being responsible for the damage.

In common with other turf chemicals fungicides must be stored in a dry place with restricted access. The recording of all fungal treatments for future reference is essential to any successful turf management program.

A check of the soil pH of fine turf should be undertaken once every second year as the correct reaction has a significant influence on disease problems.

Although it has been emphasised that disease organisms affecting fine turf are most active during humid moist conditions in combination with high temperatures, there are also a number of pathogens that thrive in cold moist situations. One such example that is quite common in Victoria during winter and early spring is *Fusarium nivale*. This disease takes the form of separate brownish-coloured patches, roughly circular and enlarging to about 154mm in which the grass dies. Treatment is important immediately this condition is noted. This disease can be aggravated if *Poa annua*, which has a high susceptibility to this pathogen, forms a significant part of the composition of a fine turf area.

*Corticium fuciforme* (pink patch) is another fungus that becomes active under similar conditions and is easily recognised by the visible pink mycelium adhering to the grass blades in patches up to 30cm in diameter. This can quickly mar the appearance of a green, but fortunately it is more easily controlled than most other fungi, and the grass recovers readily after treatment.

The pathogens of *Rhizoctonia solani* (brown patch) and *Curvularia spp.* favour similar environments, and not surprisingly have been often noted together in diseased turf. They are regarded as major turf problems and must be treated with inorganic mercurial fungicides immediately. The *Rhizoctonia solani* patches are small at first but quickly enlarge under conditions of humidity and excessive surface moisture, and it is further spread by traffic of players and mowing. *Curvularia* patches are small and tan-coloured initially (not unlike dollar spot), in which the grass appears to have died. The patches spread over the turf to coalesce and cover extensive areas. Both these infections, in combination or singly, are very unsightly and damaging, particularly if the turf is in a debilitated state from another cause at the time.

In conjunction with fungicidal treatment, it is also essential to restrict applications of nitrogenous fertilisers and watering periods and, most importantly, the drainage of the turf surface must be improved.

*Pythium spp.* is a disease which most frequently attacks grass seedlings with disastrous results if the immediate climate is favourable: warm, humid and moist conditions. The effect is that the plants collapse and die in patches, and unless treatment is prompt the infection will quickly spread through a newly-sown area. This disease is commonly known as damping off, and the incidence can be reduced to a large extent by incorporating the fungicide *Zineb* into the soil before sowing, with a further application on the young grass ten days after germination, repeating the treatment in ten days if necessary.

*Marasmius oreades* (fairy rings) is a fungus that has caused disfigurement of turf for generations, and despite the advanced knowledge available for the control of most other destructive pathogens of turf, a really practical solution has not yet been formulated for the control of this problem. It is readily identified from distinct features: a circular band of stimulated grass often interspersed with toadstools, which adjoins a circular band of dead grass with healthy turf in the inner circle, and finally a mass of white mycelium throughout the top 15cm of soil which becomes extremely dry as the fungus extends outwards.

Control measures adopted in special cases involve the replacement of the affected turf and soil to a depth of 20cm with fresh material, which can be a laborious task. Probably, however, the most effective and economical method of control is the injection of a soil sterilent throughout the affected area, work that is better performed by an experienced contractor because of the hazardous nature of these chemicals.

The effect from this fungus is more often seen on fairway turf where, unless it is widespread, it is usually considered unnecessary to embark on such a costly program of control as outlined. However, where fine turf and tees are concerned it is imperative that some form of control be implemented. In the former case, an application of nitrogenous fertiliser in the spring will reduce the definition of the rings for a short time, but will not have any effect as a control on the fungus itself. In the case of putting green turf it is rarely significant, being of a subdued nature when it does occur, which indicates that the conditions do not favour its development. Before any form of chemical is applied to the affected area the dry soil must be thoroughly moistened. This can be hastened by the addition of a surfactant to the water.

*Ophiobolus graminus* (Ophiobolus patch) will attack a number of grass species. However, as far as fairway turf is concerned, it is usually *Agrostis spp.* and *Poa annua* which are the hosts. Furthermore it is seldom extensive enough to warrant treatment. On the other hand, when putting green turf is affected it can become a serious problem which must be treated as soon as the patches are noticed. These are small initially, but quickly increase to about 30cm in diameter, are bronze in colour, and become concave as the grasses die in the centre.

Excessive surface moisture is a contributing factor in its development. Moreover, its appearance on several occasions has been seen as an adverse after-effect of liming, and brought about as a result of the strongly alkaline reaction of the turf surface at this time, a connection that has also been noted in overseas scientific literature.

In chapter 11 it is recommended that light applications of limestone are preferable on fine turf, and further that a lime solution for spraying is more readily absorbed into the turf, thus it is less liable to sustain an alkaline reaction on the surface, and to attack by the fungus. Although all the greens on a course may have been treated similarly, the disease generally will only affect a minority. This situation may be determined by other localised factors.

The recommended treatment is two applications of a fungicide eight days apart, followed by an application in solution of mono-ammonium phosphate.

Because of its objectionable nature, thatch should never be allowed to materialise on putting surfaces because it creates a very favourable environment for fungi to evolve, and makes it extremely difficult to effectively reach the organisms with fungicides.

# 20

# Turf spraying methods

Most chemicals are effective for the control of the problem for which they are recommended provided certain practical conditions before and during application are observed.

The spraying apparatus must be designed to enable accurate calibration to be made for efficiency over a known area. This is governed by the speed of the unit, and the operating pressures at the jets.

As a general rule, high pressures for spraying turf are not recommended, and should approximate 275kPa at the jets.

It is important to select jets to give a fine droplet discharge in a flat fan shape, as opposed to a circular pattern, and when fitted in line on a boom they should be adjusted to be slightly offset to avoid any contact with an adjacent jet, and the boom positioned at a height from the ground so that over-lapping of discharge from jets is minimal.

The most practical and convenient position for the boom is mounted on the front of the vehicle. This enables the operator to see clearly, without having to look backwards, that jets remain free of blockages, and that the end of the boom clears any obstructions en route.

There are a number of reliable and complete spraying units which consist of a fibre glass container with a built-in agitator and a pump to supply a selected pressure through a number of jets in line.

Essential for any boom sprayer is the provision for a form of marker, which will give the operator an indication, without damaging the turf, of the limits of the previous pass to ensure accuracy of cover.

For smaller areas appropriate models are available. However, when using this method for spraying fine turf an indication of direction is vital to determine accuracy. This may take the form of a light drag following the limits of the outside jets, leaving a line on the turf which will be visible to the operator for a short period. For fairway work, because of the longer lines of travel, a more distinct indication would be necessary.

A useful dispenser attachment obviates the problem of over- or under-spraying turfed areas by issuing at regular intervals a small quantity of inert froth which remains for some minutes along the path of the spraying unit. It is advisable to colour this material.

Timing of boom spraying applications should be arranged to avoid extremes of high and low temperatures, and spraying in strong winds is never conducive to precise distribution.

Modern chemicals in use for control of turf problems are complex, and many are known to be hazardous. In the case of hormone herbicides, most cultivated plants other than grasses are at risk.

The greatest hazard exists when the concentrated material is being handled, the diluted solution being less dangerous. However, it is common practice for the operators of spraying units to be supplied with fully protective clothing, and to be directed to wear it.

After use all spraying equipment must be flushed with clean water under pressure, to dislodge any residue, especially from the jet orifices. It is important to observe this precaution especially with equipment that has been contaminated with hormone weed spray. It is more satisfactory to retain a separate unit for the purpose of controlling pests and diseases on selected garden plants.

A practical method of liquid distribution for small areas is the ejector-type distributor made on the venturi tube principle, which will syphon a concentrated solution, under pressure, from a mains water supply, discharging through a length of hose as a mixed and diluted spray. This eliminates any risk of damage to the turf by the concentrate. With a little practice an operator can become accustomed to using the hand-piece in a wide arc, thus ensuring uniform coverage by passing over the area two or three times, or until all the concentrate has been distributed. This method is satisfactory for any soluble materials including fungicides, insecticides and fertilisers.

Unless the material being applied will remain in suspension, it is necessary for a second person to be on hand to agitate the solution to prevent any accumulation at the intake, which may result in uneven distribution and possible damage to the turf.

The addition of the correct amount of a surfactant to most spray solutions will improve their efficiency, an exception being hormone herbicides into which an agent having the same effect is included during manufacture.

A responsible attitude to the use of insect and weed controlling chemicals in golf course work is of paramount importance, with every application deemed to be justifiable.

# 21

# Control of *Poa annua* in fine turf

*Poa annua* is commonly known as winter grass, annual meadow grass, or annual blue grass, all names that suggest that it will appear for a period each year and disappear at maturity. This is true only in circumstances where definite variations in growing conditions occur. On the other hand, when it invades fine turf, it will accept the intensive care and conditions provided and regenerate from seed over most of the year.

It is a grass which is known to thrive in many different climatic and soil conditions, whether or not low lying or high elevations are involved, and is recognised throughout the world by the turf industry. Although it is accepted as a suitable grass plant in some instances, seldom is it deliberately encouraged.

It will flourish in the fine turf situation where it is looked upon as an unwanted grass because of its lighter colour and distinctive white seed and other growth habits which do not allow it to blend with the selected species. More importantly, it is often the direct cause of bumpy surfaces.

Where there is a state of heavy infestation, attacks of fungous disease are often severe and more frequent than with turf that is relatively free of the grass, suggesting that *Poa annua* is an acceptable host to a number of pathogens. Because of the combined effects of these short-comings, *Poa annua* is usually seen as a scourge of fine turf grass.

*Poa annua* will tolerate frequent low-level mowing, often becoming finer-leafed as a result, but nevertheless remaining conspicuous because of its white seed-head, and lighter green leaves. Furthermore, it will thrive in a wide range of soil reaction from strongly acid to alkaline.

It is often quite obvious how readily it will adapt to conditions that have become adverse for the selected grasses by rapidly filling in bare patches or weaknesses that have developed, regardless of the fact that the sown grasses have died or are making little progress in these areas.

A large number of people who play golf and appreciate fine turf are usually fully aware of the inconsistencies of the surfaces on which they play when *Poa annua* is prevalent. Often without having any particular knowledge of other grasses, players are able to identify this grass with assurance when it mars the turf of their greens.

When putting green turf is composed largely of *Poa annua*, the balls usually roll on an erratic line, which in itself is sufficient reason for the problem to be a constant topic of discussion by players and curators alike, the latter group subscribing to the view that the ultimate goal should be to present fine turf free of *Poa annua*.

*Poa annua* is described by C.E. Hubbard in his book titled *Grasses* as a compact annual capable of continuous replacement of dying plants with new ones from seed. This capacity gives it an aggressiveness that enables it to inhibit selected bents physically, and finally numerically, a situation which is often given support by a favourable environment and certain maintenance practices.

It is quite noticeable just how *Poa annua* plants thrive when growing in loose soil, or when undisturbed in wasteland, conditions where the roots may easily expand and produce strong healthy plants with numerous coarse leaves. In such conditions individual plants often develop creeping stems with two or three rooting nodes, a deviation of habit mainly brought about by the state of soil.

Over recent years several selective chemical agents have been developed which could prove successful in suppressing this grass. Because of the wide variation in climatic and soil conditions it is advisable, before proceeding on a large scale with a new control material, to carry out trials on a small area of turf to assess results, and especially to prove that the method of application is satisfactory.

Although the judicious use of fertilisers is essential for the maintenance of fine turf, it is also important to recognise that there are certain growth elements which tend to encourage rather than inhibit *Poa annua*. The fertilisers referred to in this context include superphosphate and formulations which include a range of trace element constituents. These should be applied minimally, keeping in mind the above recommendation.

Calcium ammonium nitrate, and blood and bone are fertilisers which will stimulate *Poa annua* to a marked degree, and for this reason they should not be applied to fine turf surfaces. The important point to bear in mind is that these particular fertilisers contribute to the establishment and continued growth of strong *Poa annua* plants, often making its suppression more difficult to achieve.

In the past it was not unusual to find a high germination of *Poa annua* and other plants among the seedlings of a newly sown area. However, it is now fairly common practice before sowing to sterilise the soil with methyl bromide gas, which provides long-term control.

In the area of fine turf culture, any form of severe mechanical cultivation of the surface such as hollow tining or deep scarifying, particularly if performed in conjunction with applications of fertilisers already mentioned, will tend to increase the percentage as well as the vigour of existing *Poa annua* plants, the latter being induced mainly by the freedom the holes or grooves permit for the development of strong roots, an activity not equalled in this situation by the Agrostis species.

Any proposed method of *Poa annua* suppression in putting green turf should include about a metre of turf on the periphery.

The question of seed distribution as a result of mowing operations cannot be overlooked. For example, where fairway turf consisting of *Poa annua* adjoins the green turf, the fairway mowers should never encroach on the fine turf as they proceed. Also, as an added precaution against increasing the percentage of *Poa annua* from the seed, the grass catcher should always be in position when mowing the putting greens.

There have been a number of reports of success in controlling *Poa annua* with applications of *Endothal*. Care in applying this material is essential. Therefore, trials should be carried out so that a full assessment may be made before moving on to more valuable turf. It is hoped, with the information available, that *Endothal* will provide a solution to what has been a most vexing problem for many years in the area of fine turf.

---

*There is always an added attractiveness about fine turf when there is an absence of* **Poa annua.**

---

# 22

## Dealing with moss and algae

### Moss

There are several species of moss found often in fine turf, either affecting a complete sward with the moss filaments growing among the grass, or in patches as a dense mass to the exclusion of the grasses.

Because these plants often mar turf over a wide range of situations, the subject of control is frequently being raised and discussed by turf management. However, despite the long-standing prevalence of the problem, it remains in many ways an aspect of turf culture in which research has been minimal.

Moss incursion of turf is always favoured by conditions adverse for healthy turf grass growth. Among a number of such factors, one common to all is the constant over-supply and retention of moisture.

Difficulties associated with moss ingress are usually less significant under a cultural program which includes adequate drainage, correct fertilising, efficient mowing and watering.

There are two species of moss that often invade secondary turf: one is velvety green in colour, the other has a yellow appearance. Both species form a thick, spongy mass, a condition which is aggravated by the very nature of the turf; and both can spread quickly and become so dense that reseeding may be necessary after successful treatment.

As is recommended for any other turf problem, control measures should be implemented in the early stages of infestation.

Where shady conditions prevail, it usually follows that there will be a reduction in sunlight on the turfed area throughout the year, which is relative to the point already made regarding excessive moisture and moss growth. Therefore, wherever practical, this situation should be remedied, at least to some extent.

Other conditions often linked with moss growth include encroaching tree roots, which aggravate a lack of nutrients and fertility of the surface soil, and insufficient turbulence in the atmosphere because of nearby buildings or trees. Also, moss often appears on bare patches that have been scalped by the mower, a surface condition that must be rectified by lifting the turf and relaying to a satisfactory line for mowing. Where necessary lime should be applied to adjust the soil reaction between pH 6.0–6.5.

Under optimum conditions the spores of moss plants are dispersed by wind, and, being further assisted by foot traffic and the movement of machinery, they germinate profusely and quickly grow into a thick mass, a situation that turf grasses cannot tolerate and so quickly deteriorate unless prompt treatment is applied.

Prior to applying chemical treatment the affected turf should be aerated, scarified and raked to remove as much moss as possible. This should be followed by an application of a mixture consisting of:

| Copper sulphate | 1 part |
| Permanganate of potash | 2 parts |
| Sulphate of iron | 2 parts |

A solution made up of 280 grams of the mixture in 4.5 L of water is sufficient to cover 4 sq m.

Several days later an application of a liquid complete fertiliser is recommended. Finally, a top-dressing with good quality soil will enable reseeding, should this be necessary, to proceed to re-establish the turf.

An alternative spraying solution can be made by dissolving and applying one gram of mercuric chloride per square metre of turf. The first mixture is not as costly and is less hazardous to use than the latter, which is used extensively for fungus disease control in turf, is poisonous and corrosive, and therefore must be handled with care and mixed in appropriate containers, for example stainless steel or plastic.

Small dense patches of moss are often found dispersed throughout fine turf areas, and it is more practical to treat these by spot spraying with either solution, after which the grass will soon begin to re-cover the patches.

## Algae

Algae thrive in somewhat similar conditions to those which encourage moss growth, although in this case shade is not always a contributing factor. Excessive moisture associated with ineffective drainage of the turf surface, particularly during humid weather, provides a situation conducive to the development of algae.

Like the mosses they are simple plants often found in fine turf, such as putting greens, that has become thin and weak. However, it can occur, albeit to a lesser extent, in healthy turf.

The most common species is Nostoc, appearing as a dark and slimy objectionable scum which retards the growth of the grass, and when dry becomes a brittle skin, apparent when it is walked upon.

The optimum atmospheric conditions are more prevalent during the late summer–autumn period, a time when over-watering of putting green turf is fairly common, thus adding to a continuance of the problem when this occurs.

During such times of humid weather, the problem can be further compounded because the Nostoc species is able to retain excessive surface moisture, evaporation is minimal and the soil is usually holding excess moisture.

Though not a disease as such, it is readily controlled with the fungicide *Dithane* — the active constituent being mancozeb 80 per cent — applied as a spray, which is made more effective by adding to the solution 4 g of sulphate of iron per 1 sq m of turf. Mancozeb has effectively superseded earlier control materials.

The problem of algae can also be overcome by providing suitable conditions for healthy turf grass growth. A recurrence can be expected until the health of the affected areas is improved. This would possibly entail a greater control of irrigation, aeration and, if the growth is weak, the removal or reduction of the causes such as shade or encroaching tree roots. Also, after checking the pH apply lime as required, and follow treatment several days later by an application of a soluble complete fertiliser.

Surface correction, to provide for effective surface drainage obviating ponding, is vital for healthy turf grass production.

# 23

---

# Thatch — causes and control

---

Thatch will develop in turf of various qualities, for example tees and fairways often become affected. When it occurs in fine turf, however, it is a very real problem.

Thatch consists of a dense accumulation of above-soil stems and stolons. Partially decayed grass clippings can also contribute to its progress, and it is characterised by the formation of a spongy mass of grass that becomes impossible to mow correctly. Generally the machine will ride over the mass of thatch taking only a little of the grass blades, the bulk being pressed down to lift up again after the mower has passed, which thereby does little to remove any of the problem.

This condition in golf greens is most objectionable as it impairs the putting surface as such, and in many cases has a tendency, because of the grass canopy effect, to inhibit water penetration, thus being a direct cause of dry patches occurring in the turf.

Invariably it becomes apparent with the formation of unevenly raised patches of grass while other areas of the turf remain unaffected.

It is a problem that is more likely to arise with stoloniferous grasses, although it has been noted, albeit much less frequently, with *Agrostis tenuis* turf, particularly when top-dressing is not a regular practice.

Fine turf needs to be kept under close observation during spring and summer, the periods during which the condition is most likely to appear, the cause sought at the first sign of the problem, and steps taken to prevent the condition occurring in the future.

Recommended restorative measures require firstly that the spongy mass be entirely removed by raking, scarifying or verti-mowing the affected parts, and all debris removed before mowing with a pedestrian-type machine set at a mowing height of 5mm, repeating several times in different directions until all the thatch is removed. The resultant bare patches may appear to be beyond recovery, but with care regeneration will slowly take place. The recovery time may be assisted with careful hand-watering, plus an application of a mild nitrogenous fertiliser in solution.

Depending upon the extent of the problem, the introduction of temporary greens could prove to be beneficial to the recovery of the patches.

111

Irrespective of the steps taken to remove the thatch, care must be exercised to avoid any damage occurring to the surface beneath which would in turn impair the grass roots from which new shoots must emerge, thus reducing the prospects for regrowth.

As the recommended treatment is necessarily severe any plan to proceed with such work during hot weather must be carefully considered. Autumn is the most suitable time particularly if reseeding of the patches is necessary.

Although, as already indicated, the grass species may contribute to thatch formation, it is primarily caused and aggravated by incorrect maintenance procedures. For instance, putting green turf must always be mown in different directions, making a definite change from the previous angle. It is also important for grass clippings to be collected as they require long periods to break down, and when allowed to fall there is generally a tendency towards sponginess, often followed by pockets of thatch development.

In addition, omission of the all-important practice of top-dressing fine turf grass with soil could be a prime cause of sponginess and thatch occurrence. There is no substitute for top-dressing in fine turf maintenance, which when carried out on a regular basis contributes so much to the continuity of healthy smooth firm putting surfaces.

Any thoughts of applying top-dressing soil to thatch-affected turf, with the idea of overcoming the problem in this way would not be successful, because it is almost impossible to work the soil through the thatch barrier and into contact with the soil beneath, which is a requisite for successful top-dressing.

---

*Thatch in fine turf can be avoided with correct top-dressing procedures, and therefore should never be neglected.*

---

Part four

Fundamental course
maintenance

Golf course maintenance practices vary greatly, because of the vastly different physical characteristics of each course, as well as the financial capacity of the respective governing bodies.

The person responsible for the maintenance of a golf course, by virtue of that position, must be thoroughly experienced, having been involved in every aspect of the work at some time, and when directing the activities of staff on the course, must have an understanding of the possible difficulties that may be encountered when the various tasks are being executed.

*The manager must always take full responsibility for any errors committed by personnel.*

# 24

# General maintenance

There are certain tasks in golf course work that constitute a significant part of overall maintenance, and for this reason must be performed with expertise.

For instance, divot marks on a golf course are obvious and always taking place, therefore it is essential that they be repaired at regular intervals. Mainly because of their diversity of cast and range mechanisation has not so far been established in this area. The method usually employed is for each person to carry clean sandy soil in a bucket from a supply vehicle, dropping just sufficient in each divot cut, and levelling it over with a foot movement. It is imperative that the soil be free of any pieces of impervious substances which could cause damage to mowers.

Over-filling divots with soil is not recommended, particularly when repairing tees where the objective is to produce a neat finish, and may be more readily achieved if the staff wear smooth-soled footwear for these duties.

Although replacement of divots is part of golf-course etiquette, players are often frustrated in their efforts as the turf will disintegrate in many conditions.

Repeated over-filling of divot marks on tees eventually leads to uneven surfaces requiring special maintenance to overcome the problem. On the other hand, when the practice is to slightly under-fill the marks and brush the work over with a light switch, the uniformity of the surface will be retained over a much longer period. To fully complete the task all pieces of turf scattered throughout the tee area must be collected.

Tee maintenance may be relieved by close attention to re-positioning the markers before the wear becomes extreme. The new position must always leave sufficient space or be far enough away to avoid any merging of the two lines of divots which could extend the worn area unnecessarily.

The depth and shape of ball marks vary, from surface bruising which requires little correction, to the deep unsightly mark, both of which indicate clearly the degree of firmness or otherwise of the turf.

In the case of the deeply cut mark where the back of the mark is usually forced up, removing a small piece of turf at the same time, a neat repair is a difficult procedure.

Many players endeavour to level ball marks as they occur by using the sole of their putter; in some cases they are provided with a small metal tool for the purpose. It is quite incorrect for a player to draw a golf shoe over the mark.

Regular repairs should be carried out by staff wearing smooth-soled footwear, and in each case drawing the sole firmly back against the line of play, an action that will replace most of the disturbed turf, and finally using a sharp metal blade 6mm wide, slightly bent for leverage, to make smooth any remaining part of the mark.

Divot marks on fairways are treated in the same manner as those on tees, but because of the extensive areas it is more practical to employ a number of the staff to walk in line 3m apart, thereby repairing the marks in broad widths as they move across the fairway. It is important to have on hand for this work a quantity of clean soil to which a complete fertiliser has been added.

Though siting of the holes in the putting greens is explained in some detail in chapter 27, it cannot be over-emphasised just how important it is for this operation to be performed with expertise at all times.

New positions must be cut before wear occurs near the hole, the worst damage always being about 30cm from the hole. This often creates a slight rise in the turf on the actual perimeter of the hole, which does not in any way assist the holing of the short putt.

When selecting a place for the hole, it is advisable to first stand the hole-cutter on the turf and well away from the previous position, then to look at the point from several directions from a distance of about 5m to ascertain that it is in a flat area or plane, 1.5 m away from slopes or rises, and not less than 6 m from the edge of the green preparatory to striking the cutter.

It is vital for the piece of change-over turf to be fitted exactly level to the adjacent

A heavy frost during August, and all the necessary equipment on hand to reposition the holes and flags before commencement of play.

turf, and, without using excessive force, made firm enough to remain thus if stepped on.

In certain aspects, the holes are subject to definition in the official rules of golf, which must be understood and observed by maintenance personnel.

Another item of maintenance which contributes in no small way towards good grooming of a course concerns tidiness of trees and plantations. This usually means the removal of dead and fallen branches and excessive debris on the ground, and the collection of small litter that has been dropped or reached the course in some way.

With such a wide selection of machines presently available, mowing between trees and shrubs is now performed with little difficulty, although in many instances the operator, in avoiding damaging machine or plants, must leave conspicuous fringes of long grass which require the use of a smaller mower or hand-tools.

When mowing greens and tees under certain wet conditions, the grass fragments often have a tendency to build on or cling to the machine frame, reaching a stage when they drop off in clumps along each pass and must be swept away with a light switch to ensure a clean finish to the work.

It is important that a system of vehicular tracks be established through the rough, and passing within close proximity to all greens and tees to enable traffic on the fairways, with the exception of mowers, to be kept to a minimum. Vehicular traffic over fairways is best discouraged at all times, particularly on good quality turf, as it is here that wheel impressions can be most noticeable; also when the turf is in a dry condition they can be more enduring and objectionable as they criss-cross in all directions.

Where members of the staff are proceeding to certain points with mowers or other machines, they should keep to the sides of fairways wherever possible, and cross at a point where the tracks will be less likely to mar the appearance of the turf.

Any operator engaged in mowing routines that affect greens, tees or fairways should be instructed to carefully retain the outlines as established by the designer.

The importance of operating power machinery with care and with an alertness for personal safety cannot be stressed too highly. It is equally important that hand tools such as shovels, spades, rakes, axes, hoes, etc. receive due care and attention, and that they are always handled with regard to safety, cleaned and oiled after use, and returned to the appropriate place in the tool-room.

The responsibility for maintaining records must be accepted by the person in charge, and not delegated to anyone else. Time must be found, if not in actual working hours, then later and on a daily basis.

It is necessary for the following items to be included in the Register:

- A diary covering the duties of each member of the staff in a concise form, noting any extra payment applicable to each day.
- A separate book in which the treatment applied to each green, tee, and fairway may be noted and understood at a glance.
- The date, purchase price, and the supplier's name of any item of equipment, and also a note of major repairs, and parts replaced in any unit.
- A log book for each mowing unit, and other vehicles to record work hours, oil changes etc. With such information at hand it is then convenient to provide the governing body with reliable data promptly if requested, or to state accurate figures when requisitioning for a new machine.
- An up-to-date inventory of all equipment in the course manager's care.
- All fertilisers, chemicals, etc. on hand catalogued periodically.

- Chemicals required for pest, weed and similar controls stored in special rooms fitted with exhaust fans, and used for this purpose only.
- Hand tools branded with the employer's initials for identification, located always in a safe manner when stored, and readily available as required.

As weather conditions govern work preparations to a large extent on a golf course, it is advisable to have on hand a barometer, a rain gauge and recording chart.

The importance of keeping in touch with all relevant literature cannot be over-emphasised, whether it concerns a new weedicide, a mower attachment, or a recently developed grass seed, the potential should be evaluated.

As mowing machines are the most frequently used units, it is essential to stock any duplicates that may be required at short notice. It is also important for instruction and spare parts books as supplied with any new machine to be carefully filed for reference.

It is always an asset to have a soil testing kit on hand to enable the turf manager to check the pH of the greens periodically for any change that may be occurring.

Where underground water is being used on turf, samples should be submitted for chemical analysis, and the subsequent report and advice carefully studied.

The machinery and workshop area of a golf course is often a place where facilities require to be updated from time to time, particularly as more valuable mechanical units are acquired, and security becomes of greater importance. A regard to cleanliness in this area is also recommended, with a hard dust-free surface where the machinery is housed and serviced. As the machines are operated in relatively clean conditions on the turf, similar conditions should continue into the immediate storage area, for practical and economical reasons.

Contingency planning for large maintenance works, or proposed golfing events is important if they are to be successful, for example, correct timing of top-dressing, weed control measures, and fertiliser applications is essential.

---

*If the elementary tasks on a golf course are well done, then assuredly the more complex maintenance will be likewise.*

---

# 25

# Bunker maintenance

Many problems associated with bunkers may be avoided by understanding the soil properties involved in their formation, and making necessary corrections. These often include anticipating drainage difficulties.

The courses that are built on sandy country often have bunkers and grassy hollows formed below the normal surface without experiencing drainage problems, even under the most extreme weather conditions.

The most important factor to be observed with bunkers is the installation and maintenance of drainage, where necessary, to remove excess water with reasonable efficiency and speed. In some circumstances it is preferable for bunkers to be self-draining as well as having agricultural piping installed. This is achieved by maintaining a minimum of fall on the floor of the bunker to avoid removal of sand or scouring during heavy rain, and lowering the edge at one point to allow the water to flow slowly to the turf beyond.

Maintenance may be further assisted in these situations if bunkers are shallow and constructed slightly above the natural terrain to facilitate overall drainage, particularly the discharge from agricultural piping.

When agricultural piping is to be laid in bunkers the base soil should be formed with a definite fall to the centre, resembling a flattened V to take the piping, which is then covered with 9.5mm gravel and extending over the bunker, finally being overlaid with 75mm thickness of fine sand. It is important for the gravel to be graded from 50mm at the sides, forming a slight hollow through the centre, and at the same time allowing a greater depth of gravel to cover the piping.

Bunker upkeep must always be regarded as being equally important with any other maintenance on the course, and should include frequent raking, weed control and sand replacement.

In all cases, a strip of firm or unraked sand about 30–45cm wide, following the bunker outline, should be retained to allow the balls to roll away from the lip to a fair lie. A vertical lip about 50mm deep must be preserved on those sections of the bunker edge that will ensure that some difficulty is maintained for all shots played towards the hole. A lip on the remainder is not important.

Rules must be formulated to suit individual cases for the elimination of unfair lies

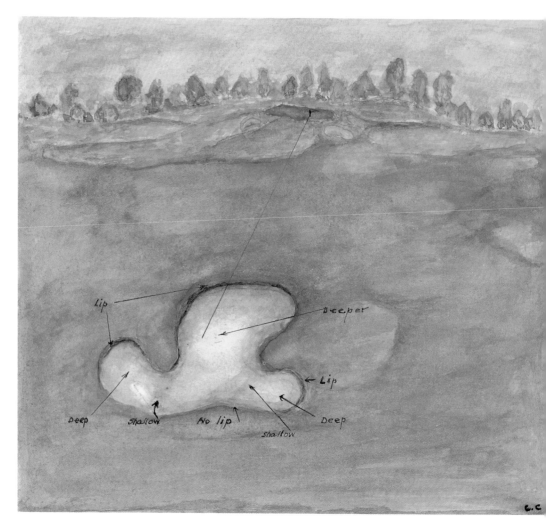

Illustrating bunker conformation that will allow balls to roll to a playable lie.

during the course of normal maintenance. These often arise through extreme weather conditions or when regular upkeep has been deferred for some reason.

Mechanical bunker raking is now a fairly general practice, wherever the total area warrants the use of these machines, and a competent operator can perform this work more thoroughly and quickly than previously. However, a hand rake should be carried on the machine for the operator to touch up any minor imperfections in the work. Operator efficiency can usually be gauged by the lack of wheel tracks and ridging remaining in the finished work.

A further useful function of mechanical rakes is the control of many weeds by their regular use in bunkers.

Where hand-raking is the usual practice, some form of light scarifying is usually indicated, especially if the sand has a tendency to harden. Furthermore, where this is the case bunker machines do not perform with nearly the same degree of efficiency when operating in the coarser sands.

Bunker edges should be neatly and lightly trimmed and grasses encroaching into the sand removed. The final effect should be neat and natural in appearance, as opposed to the severely artificial style that may be created by using a sharp knife or shovel edge. Any tendency to cut too deeply into the grass forming the edge with an implement must always be avoided.

Chemical weed control of bunkers should be able to eliminate most hand-work. The chemical selected should not cause damage to the surrounding fine turf when sand is displaced by shots played, or similarly when it adheres to shoes. Far less restrictive measures can apply in the case of fairway bunkers.

When applying weedicides to bunkers calm weather is preferable. Also a low working pressure to minimise drift on to the turf is important. As an additional precaution, a guard should be fitted to partially cover any jet that will pass close to the turfed edges, which should also be designed to prevent spray from being applied directly to the actual lips or edges.

Where broad-leafed type weeds are present a selective hormone weedicide may be used. However, if grasses are involved an appropriate eradicator must be applied. The addition of a surfactant, or wetting agent, to most spraying solutions particularly improves their efficiency with weed control in bunkers where it is essential to provide an effective coverage of all plants. To achieve the best results the soil or sand in the bunkers must be moist before applying any control solution.

Turfed tongues and pathways extending into bunkers form an important part of the design and assist players to step in and out. Because of their location, they need special attention wherever they are outside the scope of fertiliser distributors, weed sprayers and irrigation. Regular applications of fertilisers by hand-broadcasting during winter and spring can be most beneficial to turf in such circumstances. If for any reason these small areas of turf become badly impaired returfing during the autumn is usually the best solution, receiving any after-care necessary until fully established.

---

*Hazards are an essential part of the course and should be maintained accordingly.*

---

# 26

# Mowers and mowing techniques

The average total area of a golf course is approximately 45 hectares, and of this about 90 per cent is mown. Therefore, in a maintenance schedule that is fundamentally 'grow and mow', mowing expertise is central. Add to this the prime costs and maintenance of the wide range of machines and prime-movers required and mowing constitutes a substantial component of the running costs of a golf course.

Mowing of fine turf grass is an acquired skill and, whether on putting greens or other types of turf, must not be regarded at any time as being only a question of operating a mower over an area in as short a time as possible. It is important that an operator try to mow in straight lines with a minimum of over-lap, which becomes more difficult should a curved line be allowed to form the pattern, and with regular changes in direction to include all points of the compass.

The sophisticated mowing machines of today are a far cry from the earlier mowers used on putting greens. Some of the more objectionable features of old-fashioned mowers were the excessive weight badly distributed, and exposed sprockets and chains. Also, the slowly revolving cutting cylinder resulted in a miniature but noticeable corrugated effect which caused the balls to lift and deviate from the line. Over latter years, however, manufacturers have incorporated significant improvements in mower design and construction. Considerable thought has been given particularly to the design of the cutting cylinder which, in most cases, has a high speed ratio to give maximum revolutions over a given distance, a feature that is vital for a suitable finish on putting greens.

The modern mower has a lower centre of gravity giving the operator better control, and is lighter, which also benefits the operator engaged in hours of mowing. Consequently, such a machine is less liable to cause or increase turf compaction in the long term.

Some years ago a mower of unconventional design was imported from the USA, and it was immediately apparent that all the requisites most desirable in a machine for high class mowing of fine turf had been met. It introduced for the first time a floating cutting unit with freedom to pivot and thus mow precisely over surface conformations. The cutting unit can be very simply detached from the main assembly for convenient adjustments and cleaning. It has an excellent transmission, a cutting width of 533mm, and is much lighter than mowers of similar width.

Some manufacturers include a steel brush as an accessory for attaching to the front of the machine. This is very useful for removing heavy growth, particularly if taken on a double cut, that is the mower is returned in each case over the previous pass until the area is completed. In addition, mower brushing in this manner produces a significant improvement in texture by inhibiting grainy growth, a habit so often associated with bent species.

It is necessary to raise the brush attachment clear of the turf when finally mowing the perimeter of a putting green to avoid being unduly severe along the line where the machine turns.

Providing staff are available and other factors permit, frequent mowing of fine turf has a beneficial effect, improving the texture and evenness of the putting surface. Under normal conditions, however, and bearing in mind the necessity to avoid over stimulation of the turf, it should be possible to present good putting surfaces by mowing three times weekly.

An exception to this would arise when preparing for a special occasion. If upon close examination of grass clippings differences in the length of the pieces is apparent, this will indicate a variation in the growth of the leaves, and daily mowing will be necessary to maintain an ideal putting surface. Furthermore, should there be dew on the turf, mowing is the most efficient method of removing it before play begins.

If turf is wet with dew following top-dressing and before the grasses have grown through evenly, it is usually necessary to lightly water the surface by hand before mowing to avoid leaving a messy finish, or alternatively to defer the mowing until the dew has dried off completely and naturally.

With two particular exceptions, the grass catcher should always be used, and the grass never allowed to over-flow back into the cutter assembly. The first is mowing after top-dressing, providing suitable conditions prevail. Also at this time the mowers should be raised and only returned to the normal cutting height when the surfaces are again fully grassed. The second occurs immediately after applying fertilisers or chemicals, and is to avoid removing a percentage of the materials with the clippings.

In extreme weather conditions, and during dry or droughty periods, the stress on the turf can be relieved greatly by slightly raising the cutting height.

The occurrence overnight of freezing temperatures leaves a deposit of frost which often persists until about mid-morning, presenting an entirely different problem in relation to mowing fine turf grass. It is always advisable in these conditions to wait until the frost begins to liquefy, as any earlier activity on the turf will cause the frost to form into pieces of ice, which remain on the turf for very much longer than the frost.

When a mower is adjusted correctly, it is at a very delicate setting and contact with any hard material while in gear or stationary, will usually cause damage. It is therefore important always for an operator to be alert for any substance that may have, accidentally or otherwise, been left in the line of travel.

As a general guide, cutting cylinders should be adjusted as lightly as possible to sever a double thickness of newsprint. A setting of any greater tension is excessive and not in the best interests of the machine. To carry out this adjustment the engine must be stopped and the spark plug disconnected, the cylinder turned by hand and corrected to cut the paper cleanly at several points along the length of the cylinder, a detail which often requires checking during a mowing schedule.

Machines intended for mowing putting greens or similar turf should be retained for this purpose only.

As far as possible an operator should be permitted to use and accept responsibility for the maintenance of one machine, which would include the required service for an immediate start whenever the next assignment may be allocated.

Because of the normal wear which occurs between cutting blade and cylinder, a check of the standard mowing height is required periodically, and if necessary a correction made. An incorrectly adjusted mower on the one hand will mar the appearance and putting qualities of the best turf. So, conversely, will turf of a lower standard when mown well appear to be of a higher order.

One of the most important points to look for when choosing a mower for fine turf is the spacing of the clip. Providing the cutter assembly is in good mechanical condition, this should be indiscernible, especially when viewed at right angles to the direction of travel.

Any mower that is to be used on fine turf must be designed to deflect all cut grass into the catcher, thereby leaving a perfectly clean finish under all conditions. Before purchasing a mower for fine turf, a trial carried out when the turf is wet with dew or rain will indicate whether the machine is efficient in this regard. Any mower that leaves droppings of accumulated cuttings along each pass, requiring extra time to dispose of, can be regarded as defective in design. It is practical and economical to mow putting greens first thing in the morning. At this time the turf is often wet with dew, and it would be frustrating to have machines on the course with such a shortcoming.

In the operation of pedestrian-type mowers on putting greens shoes with deeply-patterned soles should be avoided in favour of smooth-soled footwear.

Efficient mowing of good firm turf with correctly adjusted machines should, as far as possible, be completed with a minimum of mower definition. To enable accurate adjustments to be made, it is necessary to use a steel gauge long enough to reach over the front and rear rollers with a machine screw and lock nut projecting through the centre. This can then contact the cutting cylinder at the height desired when the screw is held against the edge of the cutting plate. It is usually practical to retain several such gauges set as required for the different heights of mowing.

Wear takes places on the cutting plate in the form of a bevel which gradually widens and should, if adjustments are always made correctly, remain parallel as the wearing process continues.

If a mower tends to leave a rippled or wavy finish, or appears to be cutting lower on one side after correct adjustments to the cylinder have been made, the problem may be traced to worn bearings or loose frame-bolts. It is vital that ball bearings supporting the rollers and cutting cylinder be retained in perfect order. Under certain damp conditions a wavy finish may result from cut grass adhering to the rollers, which should be cleaned off at intervals to avoid a heavy build-up.

Through a period of normal use the cutting plate eventually reaches the point when it is essential for it to be replaced. The replacement must be made before contact is lost with the special steel that forms the lip of the plate, because once wear is permitted beyond this point distinct irregularities form on the edges of the cutting cylinder blades, which will then require more than normal grinding to restore.

The cutting plate must be replaced without delay when it is obvious that the bevel is running from narrow to wider. This indicates that the machine has been operating after maladjustments or damage has taken place, and it must be assumed that the tendency will be to reproduce a similar tapering pattern to the cutting cylinder, with consequent misalignment of the machine, which in turn will result in an uneven finish to the surface.

Before attempting to fit a new cutting plate in a normal situation, the cutting cylinder should be removed for minimal precision grinding, so after re-assembly there will be perfect contact between plate edge and cylinder over the full width. When a mowing unit is damaged during a work period, it is usually advisable to return it to the workshop for attention. Greater damage often results if an operator continues with a faulty machine, and the mowing is affected.

Mowing units are constantly being improved both in design and mechanically. The most recent are essentially robust with maximum protection against the entry of dust and other waste plus fine and accurate adjustments readily accessible to the operator.

The single mowing unit has been superseded by 'ride on' triplex combinations for all work on greens and tees. Triplex mowers for putting greens were developed in the USA and are presently proving popular in Australia, the main reason probably being that they enable a definite reduction to be made in the labour required for mowing putting greens.

There has been some objective criticism of triplex machines when used constantly on putting greens, mostly from overseas where experience has been gained over a much longer period. In Victoria, there have been instances where a wheel track has developed inside the perimeter of the green, because of the machine being continually forced into this line of travel when making a final clean-up of unmown segments of turf, which would not apply when mowing the body of the green. Also, in many cases where triplex mowing and regular coring are common on the greens, the turf in question appears to be more subject to wheel tracking than uncored turf.

Maintenance costs on a triplex machine, in most cases, would be comparable to the aggregate costs on three mowers in use on putting greens in the former manner.

Advantages are apparent also with the advent of manoeuvrable ride-on mowers for the tees, which are contributing to reduced turf maintenance expenditure.

There are also on the market several makes of excellent hydraulically operated gang mowers for fairways. However, any saving in hours of labour in this area would be minimal by comparison as gang mowers have been part of the scene in Australia for many years. Nevertheless the adjustments and hydraulic application to each unit makes the modern gang mower far superior to the earlier types and contributes towards better mowing and easier control.

It is important that the tees be mown with care, and to a similar recommendation for putting greens, by mowing with a change in direction on each occasion, irrespective of the type of machine in use.

In certain growth conditions an objectionable rippled effect can occur on tees and fairways, which may be more aptly described as waves running at right angles to the direction of travel. This kind of formation usually originates from a fault in the mower becoming more pronounced as subsequent mowing follows the same line. The problem may be overcome firstly by checking the bearings of the cutter and roller assemblies, and secondly by mowing several times across or at right angles to the ripple lines.

Fairways constitute the most extensive and conspicuous areas of turf on a golf course and depend largely upon the expertise with which the mowing is performed to make or mar the overall presentation of the course. Gang mowers for fairways usually consist of either five or seven units, each contributing to a swathe, which makes it essential for the cutting heights to correspond precisely, in order that the gang appears to perform as one mower.

A separate triple gang drawn with a light tractor can prove well worthwhile, its function being to mow the verges of greens and tees. It is preferable to set this

Stipa species on a bunker edge on the 12th hole, West Course. Note transition from fairway to rough.

assembly slightly lower than the fairway gang in order to graduate the mowing from greens to fairways, and at the same time relieve the fairway machine of the intricate mowing so often required in these areas.

As already stated with regard to other types of mowers, the adjustment of cutting cylinder to cutting plate must never be unduly tight, which is particularly important in the case of mowers with land-wheel drive, in order to avoid heavy traction on the turf especially under soft conditions.

It is common for fairways to have irregular outlines, which require the operator to use care in the course of the work to ensure that officially designated lines are not altered. Although fairway mowing is generally confined to a lengthwise operation, fairway turf may be enhanced if, occasionally and when time permits, this procedure is altered to directly or diagonally mowing across the fairways. This style, when followed immediately by the usual lengthwise travel, contributes significantly to the appearance of the fairways in the final preparations for a special occasion.

Wet surface conditions during fairway mowing often cause numerous droppings of cut grass along each pass, an untidy state which may be minimised by attaching a drag chain or several light tree branches to the rear of the gang in the shape of a semi-circle. These can be removed as soon as conditions improve.

In line with other mowing operations, fairway machines must be adjusted to extreme seasonal weather conditions, for instance, the turf grasses derive some benefit when the height of cut is raised slightly during the cold slow-growing periods of the year, and equally during sustained dry, hot weather.

Providing a power outlet is in the vicinity electric mowers for fine turf offer many advantages over petrol power units, and are common to bowling greens where the

Fairway mowing with a gang mower, hydraulically operated. Note the light drag at the rear to disperse grass cuttings when mowing under wet conditions.

essential character of firm, fast and closely mown turf must always be maintained. They are available in several cutting widths, few mechanical problems arise, and they are clean and quiet in operation.

The smaller models are most suitable for moderately sized lawns, providing the area is mown regularly and before the growth becomes too heavy, and there are not too many obstacles to be negotiated with the flex.

Some time ago, a battery-operated cylinder-type mower was marketed, but despite the obvious advantages in a number of areas, it did not become popular. The weight factor, and the necessity for recharging probably hindered its acceptance at the time. Perhaps some time in the future this form of power for mowers will be developed to a point where they will prove practical in home lawn maintenance and other similar areas.

In past years control of grass through the rough and steep terrain on golf courses was, of necessity, labour intensive and time consuming. However, the rotary mower has proved to be economical and effective in this area of maintenance. The high speed of the blades results in the grass being chaffed, which usually obviates any necessity to dispose of the waste.

The smaller models, some with a grass catcher attached, are manually propelled and are very useful for mowing bunker edges, pathways and the like, which are inaccessible to larger machines. These are in demand for home gardens whose owners desire to establish a reasonably neat finish at minimum cost.

There are larger machines available with the same rotary principle, which are assembled as complete and compact units. There are also separate assemblies for a power take-off drive, which are very effective for larger areas of rough and in plantations. The actual method of mowing may consist of a single rotating blade or a series of shafts with plates to which are attached replaceable cutting blades, each system using vee-belt drive.

Periodically unfavourable conditions for mowing fairways prevail on golf courses situated on badly drained or heavy soils. Such conditions are usually the result of a spell of wet weather culminating in waterlogged soil and making conventional mowing almost impossible as the grass continues to grow. However, the problem may be relieved by temporarily utilising rotary blades off the power take-off of a light tractor, which will provide a limited control of growth and also improve playing conditions.

On a somewhat similar basis, a new development in gang mower design has been introduced to Australia, and is sold as a complete and compact assembly, combining a tractor and mowing units fitted with a complete hydraulic system for lifting and lowering each mowing unit as required during travel, and which also drives the cutting cylinders, with all controls effective from the driving position. This means that while in operation the mowing units are virtually being towed, and to facilitate this movement they are fitted with steel skids, taking the place of land-driven wheels, an advantage in any mowing situation but more particularly when soft turf conditions prevail.

In looking back at the exceptional difficulties experienced when trying to mow grass on areas where strong growth persisted, and the progression through hand-scythes and reciprocating horse- and power-driven blades, any positive opinion reached must inevitably focus on the efficiency of the present-day rotary mowing through a vertical shaft, which has revolutionised the control of secondary grass, through long thick growths, and within reason, enabled mowing over uneven terrain. These advances in technique have greatly reduced the arduousness of the work which now requires only a fraction of the time, and provides a cleaner and neater finish.

# 27

# Course preparation for major tournaments

It should be possible, with certain reservations, to play an important event on a championship course at short notice. Obviously there would be less effort required to meet a deadline if a high standard of maintenance on the course were the usual practice.

An alteration to the course, or some similar project, could perhaps create a time problem, if for some reason short notice only is given. However, it is more usual for the official negotiations regarding the course, competitors, and visitors to take place as early as twelve months beforehand, which gives the course manager ample time for all the work involved to be performed in correct sequence.

An early meeting and course inspection should be arranged between the green committee and the curator so that a program of any earth or turf works deemed necessary may be planned and given priority accordingly. Any such project must reach maturity before the event, and certainly not appear to have been done for the occasion. Final agreement on undertakings of this nature will often require some further discussion.

Planning for special occasions must always be regarded as being a joint effort by club officials and links staff. The course manager must take responsibility for every item from the entrance gates and so on throughout the course to see that it is all presented in first class condition in accordance with the objective of providing eighteen unblemished greens, together with good tees and fairways.

Where large numbers of visitors are expected, it is vital for positive advice and direction to be given on all matters relating to facilities for the public, such as additional points of entry, location of catering and toilets, and tree clearance for pathways, etc. so the spectators have freedom to move from tee or green on any hole. If large numbers of visitors are expected, direction indicators to all points of interest on the course are always appreciated. Although it is important that as few tasks as possible in this area are left to the last days, there must necessarily be work that cannot be attempted until several days before the start of the competition and these requirements must be carefully noted.

It is essential to impose strict controls on all vehicles being used in the installation of services, etc. on the course to prevent objectionable wheel marks being seen over the fairways, especially on television film, which would otherwise depict perfect turf. Television cameras have a most discerning exactness, and convey every imperfection in the turf, whatever the cause.

With any constructional changes that may have been decided upon now proceeding, the next step in the plan may include weed control on a thoroughly wide basis and, in the case of the fairways, it should be in hand before distribution of fertiliser, thereby permitting any temporary ill-effects from the weedicide to grow out well in advance.

The extreme importance of timing must be noted, and the various operations must be studied in accordance with the time of year the event is scheduled to take place. Obviously, if the meeting is to be held in the winter — June to August — the growing process will then take longer than in springtime. Also in the cooler period there may be very different problems to solve than would be encountered in course preparations at any other time of the year.

The application of fertilisers to the fairways in the springtime requires some thought as, ideally, the maximum response should occur about two weeks before so that a more moderate growth is realised at the actual time of the event. This situation will enable more efficient mowing of the fairways than could be expected during the flush of growth.

Another important factor to be considered is the number of days of competition involved, as special daily maintenance must be taken into account over whatever period is necessary, and the course preparations must be completed to the desired standard a week before the tournament begins.

At this time competitors are arriving for practice and it then becomes increasingly difficult for the staff members to carry out their tasks without interruptions. Furthermore, the competitors appreciate being able to play the course as it will be, and so gain experience of the speed and intricacies of the putting surfaces, as well as the general strategic characteristics of the layout.

The most fundamental principle in the art of greenkeeping must be that the greens take precedence, therefore careful and frequent inspections by the curator are necessary to detect and arrest any surface problem at the outset. Approximately eight weeks before the competition begins the turf on the immediate verges of the greens, together with the aprons or approach areas should be examined and any imperfect turf replaced.

When preparations are complete the greens will be closely mown with the adjacent turf graduating to the higher mown turf of the fairways, which is achieved by mowing an area extending about 14 m forward, and at a slightly higher level, as frequently as necessary to maintain the turf at a good standard, and must also include a reducing width of similar turf following the perimeter of the green.

The mowing described should be designed to enable the fairway mowing to be neatly completed with facility, without encroaching on the specially mown turf close to the greens.

Finally, a top-dressing with soil may be necessary to produce turf of a character intermediate between green and fairway.

The tees must receive special attention to include the maintenance of vigorous growth, with weed control and top-dressing the turf to provide flat and even surfaces.

Some practical means must be employed to preserve sufficient turf on each tee at the stipulated distance to cover the competition.

Points for all practice by the competitors must be designated and enforced outside these special areas.

Divots will usually be of a less prominent nature if the mowers are adjusted to a height to retain some depth in the turf.

As the start of the tournament draws nearer mowing procedures become more important, and nowhere is this more applicable than to the fairways where mowing frequency will contribute greatly to the final effect. Extra time will also be required for cross mowing to perfect the condition of the turf before the gallery control ropes are staked out, as the complete mowing of the fairways becomes difficult once these restrictions are applied.

Where the preparations concern an autumn or springtime competition, the top-dressing compost for the greens must be prepared about two months beforehand for application six weeks ahead of the opening day. Top-dressing of the tees and approaches to the greens should be arranged to take place prior to the greens.

When the competition is planned to take place during the winter, then possibly top-dressing of the greens with soil beforehand could be omitted in favour of a suitable liquid fertiliser application.

From a practical point of view, it is advisable to have on hand spare sets of equipment such as hole cups, flag sticks, numbered flags, and tee markers, etc. ready to arrange on the course at any time.

Usually as the first day of the competition approaches, the staff become fully aware of the importance and urgency of such an occasion, and that there must inevitably be changes to the usual working hours over the period of the meeting. Work must begin at a time that will allow all daily preparations to be completed ahead of the first players on the course, and also cover any unforeseen delays such as may occur through faults in mechanical units. It is always a good policy to have a little spare time to cope with emergencies should they arise. During the tournament, all mowing duties should be carried out before or after play, and arranged to avoid any inconvenience to the competitors.

Weather conditions play an all-important role in the success of any major event, irrespective of the time of year it takes place. If unfavourable weather occurs and affects the maintenance preparations leading up to or during the event, frustrating as it may be, it is wise to accept the situation and try to present the course in as near perfect condition as possible.

On the other hand, under favourable conditions the course preparations should be completed and maintained throughout in a manner that all may see at a glance that the turf is perfect, leaving no doubt that exciting golf will ensue.

The temperate climate of Melbourne and its environs would be acknowledged by many to be the most suitable in Australia for all-year-round culture of fine turf. Probably the most difficult time is during the summer, when extreme care is necessary to sustain the turf, mainly with the judicious use of water, over a period of about four months, often through high temperatures. Also at this time of year sudden storms are not uncommon and can cause temporary flooding. It is then that the advantages of well drained green surfaces become obvious, as play is able to continue with little delay or inconvenience to the competitors.

The bunkers should be maintained in a clean, loosely raked and defined condition throughout. Bunker edges that will cover shots to the green must have a well-formed vertical lip, grading away to the floor of the bunker. It is important, when bunkers are being prepared, to leave a band of firm unraked surface about 45cm wide to allow balls to roll away from the edges, and enable them to be played fairly to the hole.

A practice teeing ground of a suitable area for the number of competitors should be prepared in advance, mown regularly, and preserved intact until the event begins. As is the case with all tees during the competition, this area also requires daily maintenance, such as the removal of divots and the filling of the marks with soil, with a section designated for practice each day.

The practice putting green must be of a similar standard to that of the greens, so the competitors may consider any time spent in practice worthwhile. Furthermore, for its value to be fully appreciated, it is essential for the holes to be repositioned daily during the tournament.

As a result of the top-dressing the greens will reach the stage when special treatment is required with raking and combing attachments fitted to the mowers and used in various directions until a few days before the competition begins, in an effort to provide firm, fast surfaces on which the balls roll truly from any part of the greens.

With the adjacent turf of the approaches and the edges mown closely, the greens take on an appearance of vastness with the target area somewhat less obvious, an effect which may be further heightened if necessary by late applications of small quantities of liquid nitrogenous fertiliser, to blend the colour of the greens to that of the surrounding turf. At the same time the greens are not required to be highlighted with vividly green turf, as there is no real relationship between colour and true putting turf.

It must be emphasised just how important is the placing and cutting of that focal point, the hole in the green. About two weeks before the event begins, all holes should be moved to quite forward positions, especially when competitors are engaged in practice rounds. This will not create such an unusual situation, as by this time the approach areas are in good condition, and further, it will mean that most of the practice shots are pitched to this forward turf, thereby saving the important hole position turf from much traffic and ball marking.

It is advisable to keep the hole-cutting tool honed to a keen edge, and in a protective cover, for the holes to be cleanly cut each day, and with scissors on hand to make a final trim of any grass blades that may be out of place on the edge of the hole. The actual lip of the hole must not be trimmed in a manner that deviates in any way from a sharp square-edge finish.

When the hole cup is being inserted to the specified depth of 25mm below the level of the turf, there is often a tendency for the immediate turf to be forced up slightly by air pressure. To overcome this, it is necessary to include in the tool kit a flat steel plate — 220mm x 150mm x 6mm — with a handle attached, which is used to gently tap down the turf surrounding the hole before finally giving the cup setting tool one complete turn. Similarly, a flat board or steel plate, with a central hole to accept the hole cutter, and large enough for a person to stand on, will also prevent any surface movement at the edge of the hole during the operation.

The positions of the holes for each day should be planned ahead so that the new position is as far as possible from the previous setting. Any old hole sites that are noticeable prior to the tournament should be encouraged to grow out, with a weak solution of fertiliser applied just where required.

The replaced plug of turf must always be fitted, levelled and firmed meticulously to the surrounding surface, and if necessary, a little soil worked into the line of the join.

Each hole should be placed on a flat plane of not less than 2 m radius in the best turf, which should be closely inspected for any minor imperfections that may deflect a ball as it nears the hole.

When preparations for special occasions have been intensified, it is recommended that staff members or caddies, whose duties require them to walk on the

The tool kit required for a new hole setting: scissors; flat steel blade; hole cutter; cup puller with short handle; trowel; cup setter to set cup to the correct depth.

A neatly cut hole, with vertically standing flag stick.

greens, should wear plain-soled footwear to keep impairment of the surface to a minimum. This recommendation may appear to be superfluous in view of the fact that as soon as the first competitors walk on to the turf wearing spiked shoes, some effect on the surface will be obvious. Nevertheless, for such occasions, the turf should always be introduced in flawless condition, irrespective of what may occur later.

Several weeks before the event is due to start, divot marks, or any irregularities on the fairway turf, should be filled with soil, or repaired and maintained in this condition throughout.

For special tournaments it is important that daily course maintenance include such tasks as:

- Mowing greens, tees and fairways.
- Transferring tee markers to other positions.
- Repositioning the holes on the putting greens.
- Repairing divot marks on tees and fairways.
- Clearing away loose divots and other litter from tees, including practice teeing area.
- Bunker raking.
- Carefully repairing ball marks on the greens.
- Moving the holes on the practice putting green.

With the preparations completed, the tees are in good order, the fairways are evenly covered and well mown, and the greens are firm, of a consistent texture, fast and true.

On the eve of a major golf championship, or at any other time for that matter, it is always gratifying for the curator, after many weeks of planning, to present such turf quality to members, competitors and visitors.

---

*Quality putting green turf must never be too benign.*

---

# Reflections

Turf culture has been my occupational interest for 54 years, with the responsibility for developing and maintaining golf course turf over this period. It proved to be a highly sufficient, at times demanding, vocation, but certainly never an uninteresting one.

Prior to commencing at the Royal Melbourne Golf Club, I was employed for a number of years on a large state property, where I gained experience and an appreciation of turf work. I was particularly motivated towards a standard of fine turf for golf greens which would be pure, firm and fast.

For many years this type of turf has become widely known as being essential to the courses at Royal Melbourne. To me, it always appeared relevant that high quality putting greens be presented to competitors, particularly for major tournaments, irrespective of the venue. However, circumstances and conditions can make such a specification difficult to arrange.

Several weeks after I began what was to be a long association with the Royal Melbourne Golf Club, a team of women from the UK arrived in Australia in 1935 to play in the LGU championship on the East Course, a visit which created a lot of interest and attracted many visitors to the course.

The course at this time had only recently been completed and was not fully developed, with many aspects of drainage still requiring attention. Unfortunately, there was heavy and sustained rain prior to and during the meeting. I recall this as probably being the singular occasion when I felt displeased with the course preparations.

There were a number of holes affected in one way or another, major problems being bunkers holding water, and squelchy fairways. This was caused largely by stormwater being diverted from adjacent roadways. The one thing that could be done was to continuously pump, syphon and bail water from the bunkers. The large areas of the 11th and 18th fairways which were submerged, were to a large extent drained a day or two before the event began.

It was obvious from this experience just what was required, and over the next few years drains were installed to alleviate such problems as quickly as possible.

In 1937 it was decided to construct a new 7th green on the West Course, and in due course the present site was selected. The reasons for the change were the severe

135

The author.

characteristics in the formation of the old green, which was unpopular with the members. Of even greater importance was the situation at the 1st East tee and the 8th West tee, which were adjacent and the holes practically parallel, an arrangement so often criticised.

Two years later, August 1939, the Australian Open Championship was played on the West course, and once again the weather played no small part. Days of heavy rain during the weeks preceding the tournament made it difficult to finalise the preparations. Over the days of the meeting, however, there was little rain, but conditions were very trying for the competitors with a sustained cold south-westerly blowing, at times reaching gale force, plus firm, fast greens.

This meeting included the Open, Amateur, and Professional Championships as well as several other events, all played over ten consecutive days. Following the war, when play resumed in 1946, each event went to a separate venue.

During the war the links staff gradually dwindled to five with consequent deterioration in maintenance. There was an acute shortage of fertilisers for sports turf, which was in the lowest priority group. However, a poultry farmer nearby was only too pleased for me to send a truck and clean out the pens. He had been without help for some time, which was evident by the volume of manure under the perches.

The fowl manure was mixed with soil to top-dress the greens a number of times before normal supplies of fertilisers were again available.

I also had a visit from a supplier of animal manure who assured me he had regular quantities available. On enquiring further regarding its origin, I discovered that he cleaned out the cages at the zoo and, although the composition was diverse, he assured me that the manure would produce an excellent result on turf. I decided the poultry waste would be less hazardous as there is generally little variation in the analysis.

From a turf maintenance point of view, 1945 was memorable for the spectacular advance made in weed control with the initial release of selective hormone weedicides in the spring of this year. Subsequently, a series of satisfactory experiments was conducted at Royal Melbourne by the distributors of the materials.

As a result, we evolved a boom sprayer which, though not equal to present-day models, nevertheless could be drawn over the fairways applying the weedicide in wide strips and thereby, for the first time, effectively and speedily controlling many weed species — indeed a boon.

The Australian Professional Golfers Championship was held on the West course in December 1947, and attracted a large enthusiastic gallery, thus heralding a return to competitive golf. Our staff had gradually returned from duty, so that for this occasion the course was in very good order, though the final between Pickworth and Cremin was marred to some extent by heavy rain.

Water shortages over the years in the Melbourne area frequently resulted in restrictions, often severe. The winter of 1967 was unusually dry, a situation that continued throughout the spring and summer into the autumn of 1968, and resulted in the most stringent restrictions I had ever experienced.

A number of golf clubs around Melbourne had been able in previous years to provide for their own supplies. At Royal Melbourne, however, a number of attempts to locate a worthwhile underground supply had been unsuccessful since the early 1930s.

As the position continued to deteriorate, it became obvious that the objective must be to save the turf of the greens, but it was far from clear at the time if or how this could be achieved. At this crucial point both the Victoria and Woodlands Golf Clubs offered some water from their bores to augment our meagre supply. This

The short 7th on the West Course at Royal Melbourne: 135 m to an elevated green, with the unique ruggedness of native plants intervening.

undoubtedly saved the turf of the greens from possibly extinction, and certainly relieved much of my anxiety.

To gain maximum benefit from this arrangement, I obtained a polythene lining to fit a convenient bunker where a large tanker could quickly discharge and return for another fill. Other smaller tanks fitted with pumps were then filled at this point to hand-water the greens.

The outcome of all this was that ideal conditions prevailed on the composite course for the 6th World Amateur Championship which was held in October 1968.

I always derived much pleasure from being responsible for the presentation of the course at all times, particularly for those tournaments hosted by the Royal Melbourne Golf Club that relate to the world golf scene. As well as the championship already mentioned, this category would include the Australian Open Championship (3), the Australian Amateur Championship (3), the Australian Ladies Amateur Championship (2), the Ladies Commonwealth tournament and the World Cup.

There were, however, three special occasions which, in my opinion, were outstanding in interest for large numbers of golf enthusiasts. The first may not quite qualify, as it was a private match between Pickworth and Locke on the West course for members and their friends in October 1950. However, the occasion is still recalled by many because of the brilliant play, and the ability of each player to match the other shot for shot. Pickworth was out in 30 and birdied nine of the first eleven holes. Locke was out in 33 and shot a 65, but was beaten 2 and 1 by Pickworth who shot a 63. This was the first occasion Locke had played the course, and after the round he expressed his astonishment at the turf quality throughout. He was especially impressed by the 3rd hole, which he declared to be one of the world's great golf holes.

In November 1959, the Royal Melbourne composite course, as it has become known, was utilised for the first time to play the 7th Canada Cup and International

Trophy, later renamed the World Cup. This was a highlight which attracted enormous crowds from — literally — the golf world. Likewise, it was the first time that a golf event of this nature was televised in Australia, which in itself was responsible for attracting many more enthusiasts to the game.

The 20th World Cup and International Trophy Championship was again held at Royal Melbourne Golf Club on the same layout in 1972.

The third event, which occurred in 1961 on the West course, I found extremely interesting. The occasion was a match between Peter Thomson and Gary Player for a television film being made by an American film company, which visited eleven countries around the world, playing each of the series on a course considered to have notable features, and over 18 holes.

The commentator throughout was Gene Sarazen, the participants outstanding players in each case, and each program was of one hour duration when complete. The filming entailed four long days of activity with everyone involved being subject to the directors' supervision, shots being played only when everyone was in position for shooting, and the light correct.

In many cases it was necessary to camouflage camera crews with tree branches. This required considerable time, particularly where a camera was located on a very high platform to enable a certain shot to be depicted properly.

Having prepared a golf course for many special occasions, the course manager comes to realise that, in common with many other sports, the competitors are the stars as far as the many interested spectators are concerned. However, I believe that most visitors to tournaments do notice the features and general presentation of a golf course, and also that the players appreciate strategic as well as turf qualities as factors which contribute to the success of a golf meeting.

---

*You cannot just let it happen; you must make it happen.*

---

# Annual course maintenance program

Key: **1** Fertilisers  **2** Weed control  **3** Insect pests  **4** Other undertakings

## Appendix 1: Greens, summer

**1** Apply a complete liquid formulation at half recommended strength when necessary.

**2** Avoid the use of weedicides, unless it becomes necessary.
When weeds are not too numerous in fine turf, hand-weeding is always an alternative.

**3** Observe closely for Argentine stem weevil activity in fine turf.
Apply fungicides to fine turf as a regular preventive schedule, or as a curative measure.

**4** Mowing procedures twice weekly. Raise mowers.
Move holes in greens at least once weekly.
Irrigate turf as required.
Maintain sprinklers and hoses in efficient working order.

## Appendix 2: Greens, autumn

**1** Light dressing only. Applied to promote healthy growth without over stimulation.
Prepare top-dressing soil for application during April.

**2** Apply weedicides as watering requirements of the turf taper off.

**3** Apply fungicides for disease control. Control algae; *Nostoc spp.* often prevalent, apply *Mancozeb.*

**4** Carefully estimate water requirements to a minimum. Special attention to dry patches.
Replace any turf loss.
Move holes in greens once weekly.
Repair ball marks.
Lower mower cutting height, if raised previously for summer mowing.

## Appendix 3: Greens, winter

**1** Complete fertiliser + extra potash in solution as required.

**2** The use of weedicides is not recommended during periods of slow growth.

**3** Treat Fusarium disease with fungicide as soon as it appears.
Repeat treatment for Nostoc if necessary, refer to autumn recommendation.

**4** Mow twice weekly at lower level.
Ball marks may require regular attention.
Move holes in greens to avoid turf wear, which is often decided by the number of players, and in accord with weather conditions.

## Appendix 4: Greens, spring

**1** Prepare top-dressing soil and apply during favourable weather.

**2** Use weedicides where necessary, and before the top-dressing is applied.

**3** Apply an insecticide to prevent attacks by pests during the months ahead.
Follow up treatment of Fusarium disease.

**4** If applicable use mower attachments to remove excessive growth before top-dressing turf.
Move holes in greens twice weekly.
Attention to ball marks.
Check sprinklers and hoses before they are put into use.

## Appendix 5: Fairways, summer

**1** Not required.

**2** Not required.

**3** Argentine stem weevil must be treated with an insecticide immediately any damage becomes apparent, particularly to the turf in the vicinity of the greens.

**4** Irrigate if a suitable system is operative.
It is important when couch is the dominant grass to use water judiciously.
On the other hand, if such a system is not available an effort should be made to at least sustain the turf of the approaches and verges of the greens with special attention.

## Appendix 6: Fairways, autumn

**1** Complete fertiliser 2–2–1. Distribute during April.

**2** Implement *Paspallum dilatatum* control. When plants are scattered spot-spraying or hand-digging will give satisfactory results.
As there is no other selective method of treating this grass, methyl bromide gas would be the most effective material for control where there exists a high degree of infestation.
Early autumn application is recommended.

**3** Cockchafers or underground grass grubs causing damage to the turf may be effectively controlled by spraying with a mixture of Lindane + DDT.*

**4** Regular mowing is generally required. Adjust mowing height to accord with growth response, usually a medium setting.
Inspect drains; clear inlets, outlets and sediment pits.

* The use of DDT is now prohibited.

## Appendix 7: Fairways, winter

**1** Not required.

**2** Late winter, selective overall spray for control of broad-leafed weeds.

**3** Repeat application of insecticide if damage to turf continues.

**4** Lime turf to comply with advice following laboratory soil test.
Apply lime–superphosphate 1.1 mixture alternating with the lime application at two- or three-year intervals, as an aid towards the retention of a satisfactory soil reaction.
Fill divots with soil.

## Appendix 8: Fairways, spring

**1** Early spring, distribute a mixture of:
calcium ammonium nitrate
superphosphate
potash

**2** Only where required.

**3** Late spring, apply an insecticide overall consisting of DDT* + Lindane every alternate year.

**4** Usually heavy and regular growth throughout this season, which will require constant attention to mowing procedures, and machinery.
Fill divots with soil twice during season.

* See above.

## Appendix 9: Tees, summer

**1** As is necessary to maintain forward growth.

**2** Apply weedicide to retain turf in weed free condition.
Remove paspallum plants.

**3** Any turf damage apparent, suspect the Argentine stem weevil, and promptly treat with an insecticide.

**4** Water regularly.
Mow once weekly.
Fill divot marks with soil and seed. Move teeing positions as required to avoid excessive wear of the turf.

## Appendix 10: Tees, autumn

**1** Include with fairway fertiliser application.

**2** Implement weed control.

**3** Apply insecticide if there is any pest activity apparent.

**4** Where there is surface unevenness, lift turf and re-lay to a flat plane, and top-dress.
Water turf as required.
Mow once weekly.
Fill divot marks with soil.
Reposition tee markers.

## Appendix 11: Tees, winter

**1** Apply complete fertiliser to maintain growth throughout this season.

**2** Not required.

**3** Control Fusarium disease promptly.

**4** Trench and prune encroaching tree roots.
  Continue to rectify uneven surfaces.
  Fill divots with soil once weekly.
  Mow once weekly.
  Reposition tee markers whenever necessary to prevent undue wear occurring.

## Appendix 12: Tees, spring

**1** Include in fairway application.

**2** Use selective weedicide for control of broad-leafed weeds.
  Remove paspallum plants, and other problem grasses.

**3** Include in fairway insecticide program.

**4** Top-dress surface with soil following fertiliser application.
  Complete pruning of tree roots encroaching into turf before the summer, and remove overhanging tree branches.
  Fill divot marks with a soil and fertiliser mixture.
  Move teeing positions as often as required.
  Mow once weekly; adjust height to a slightly lower level than usual.
  To be included in any fairway liming program.

## Appendix 13: Bunkers, summer

**1** Treatment nil.

**2** Treatment nil.

**3** Treatment nil.

**4** Rake regularly.
  Trim edges; use care with mechanical trimmers to avoid any excessive removal of the established edge.
  Replace sand to rectify unfair lies.

## Appendix 14: Bunkers, autumn

**1** Treatment nil.

**2** Where troublesome weeds and grasses have to be controlled, a liquid material should be obtained with the qualities as described in chapter 25 and if applied through medium-size jets under a low pressure, a satisfactory result should be achieved.

**3** Treatment nil.

**4** As general maintenance, rake and trim edges; when necessary scarify the bunker floors to maintain the sand in a loose condition.
  Check and clear drains.

## Appendix 15: Bunkers, winter

**1** Attention to weak turf on edges and adjacent to bunkers. Fertiliser application to increase vigour of grasses.

**2** Weeds growing in the turf of paths, tongues and edges are often inaccessible to boom spray cover, therefore, it is necessary in such cases to apply a selective control under low pressure, via a hand-lance.

**3** Treatment nil.

**4** Retain original design by returfing wherever erosion occurs. First quality turf only is recommended when rebuilding paths etc.
Upon completion of work, fertilise and top-dress with soil.
Raking to be performed regularly.

## Appendix 16: Bunkers, spring

**1** Repeat fertiliser application of any weak edge forming turf.
Calcium ammonium nitrate plus potash is recommended.

**2** Continue with weed control where required.

**3** Treatment nil.

**4** Rake, and trim edges.
Use light scarifier to maintain loose sand on the floor.

## Appendix 17: Rough and trees, summer

**1** Treatment nil.

**2** Cultivate and mulch young trees and shrubs.
Control noxious plants, e.g. blackberry, gorse (furze) and bone seed plants.

**3** Apply a dual-purpose spray as required to control insect pests and diseases affecting immature plantings.

**4** Attention to staking and ties.
Mow grass rough between fairways at a height that will produce a penalty but which will avoid balls being lost.

## Appendix 18: Rough and trees, autumn

**1** Apply blood and bone sparingly to certain young trees and shrubs; do not include native species in any fertiliser treatment.

**2** Most of the broad-leafed weeds in the rough areas are effectively covered with the boom sprayer in conjunction with the fairways application. Inaccessible places will require the use of a hand-sprayer.
Avoid spray drift to susceptible plants.

**3** Apply insecticide to any affected plants.

**4** Tree maintenance will include trimming away of low and overhanging branches, also removal of dead or broken limbs and other waste.
Mow grassy rough as recommended.
Undertake new plantings.
Trim hedges.

## Appendix 19: Rough and trees, winter

**1** Treatment nil.

**2** Proceed with the removal of all dead wood from all established plantations.
   Seal large cuts with a suitable wound dressing.

**3** Treatment not usually required.

**4** All tree growths to be cut back clear of fences and gateways.
   Trees which overhang vehicular tracks must also be removed to provide free access to all units moving through the course.

## Appendix 20: Rough and trees, spring

**1** As a general recommendation, fertiliser application to the rough areas should always be avoided, and fairway applications executed precisely to avoid any excess growth of the rough on the fairway verges.
   Fertilisers do not benefit dwarf native plants growing in the rough, ususally the effect is adverse.

**2** Cultivate young trees and shrubs.
   Eradicate bone seed plants.

**3** Spray for control of larvae of saw tooth moth on large trees, e.g. *Eucalypt spp.*

**4** Mow native plants in the rough at a high setting, once yearly in the late spring. Avoid any severe treatment of these plants.
   Where possible burn off tree waste at selected sites before the onset of the summer.

# Glossary

**Acidity or alkalinity of a soil is expressed on a scale as a pH value**  A pH of 7 is neutral and above 7 alkalinity exists; an acid reaction occurs below 7.

**Aeration of turf**  An operation performed mainly by machines designed for the purpose — to remove pieces of turf on their line of travel; greens, tees, or fairways may be quickly and effectively treated.

**Agrostis**  Species of grasses including group regarded in many areas as being most suitable for fine turf development; often referred to as bent grasses.

**Amendment**  Recommended addition to soil of material that will alter its physical properties to suit planting: coarse sand, peat, other vegetable matter, and/or lime, are often considered for this purpose.

**Apron, or approach**  Part of the fairway adjacent to front of green and not less than 6m in width gradually reducing as it extends to sides of green: this turf should be of good quality and mown accordingly.

**Artificial turf**  Recently developed synthetic material accepted as alternative turf in certain instances.

**Ball mark**  Indentation made by impact of ball on surface of green. The mark can vary considerably from bruise to depression, or removal of small piece of turf, according to condition of surface and type of shot played.

**Bed plate**  Substantial steel plate equal in length to width of mower, usually fitted between side frames; pivots to provide adjustment of bottom blade to cutting cylinder.

**Biological control**  Mainly control of insect pest by introduction into environment of its natural enemies, or parasites, often another insect.

**Bottom blade**  Stationary steel blade of good quality, with or without lip, which is accurately ground and always carefully adjusted to cylinder blades to produce even shearing cut.

**Broadcast application**  Accurate distribution of dry material over given area either by mechanical means, or by hand.

**Brushing**  Practice of mowing greens, with attached stationary steel wire brush, in several directions during periods of heavy growth; assists in improving texture and reducing surface graining.

**Casts**   Soil and plant particles excreted and left on surface by worms.

**Catcher or grass box**   Detachable metal or plastic box fitted in front of mower to collect clippings.

**Clip**   Frequency of cuts performed over a certain distance, estimated by designer of mower; most important feature of any machine to be used for greens mowing.

**Collar turf**   Narrow area of good quality turf adjoining putting surface and reducing as it extends around sides of green; usually mown slightly higher than green to avoid formation of step with adjoining fairway.

**Combing**   Comb with flexible steel tines, available as accessory to be fitted to mower in front of cutting cylinder to remove any coarse stems; when used in conjunction with **brush** has a beneficial effect on surface environment of fine turf.

**Compaction**   Condition where soil particles become dense, usually through external pressures; must be alleviated to improve health of turf.

**Coring or hollow tining**   Performed by machines which drive number of tines into turf and automatically remove and deposit small cylinders of this.

**Cross mowing**   Operation which may be performed periodically by mowing fairways across width, finally lengthwise in normal manner.

**Cultivar**   Plant of species which has desirable qualities that can be sustained under cultivation.

**Cutting cylinder**   Basic item of mower formed by series of curved blades fixed to spindle by disc to provide rigidity.

**Cutting height**   Measurement usually adjustable to manufacturer's indications on sides of machine; should be noted for reference later if changes to be made to particular setting.

**Dormancy**   Resting phase of plant during which all surface growth virtually stops; will continue until seasonal conditions are appropriate for renewed growth to begin.

**Double cut**   Special method of mowing whereby operator returns over same path until green is complete. As with normal mowing, it is important for operator to change direction on every occasion.

**Face**   That part of hazard which when constructed is described as bunker face, and which player is required to negotiate.

**Fairway**   That area between tee and green with precise outline designed by course architect, and requiring to be always mown and maintained accordingly.

**Fescue grasses**   Fine-leafed and hardy with upright growth; usually included in bent mixture where the objective is propagation of fine-textured putting surface.

**Forking**   Method of turf cultivation provided by forcing square tined fork into the turf 75mm apart.

**Grooving**   Turf cultivation by means of vertical rotating blades which cut continuous slits through turf to controlled depth.

**Hazard**   Any bunker, or permanent water within playing area.

**Herbicide**   A chemical agent having controlling effect on most forms of plant life.

**Hole-cutter**   Has an outside diameter of 106.35mm.

**Hole-cutter protector**   Hole-cutter must be kept honed, and always covered with metal protector.

**Hole-liner, or cup**   Has an outside diameter of 106.35mm.

**Lip**   About 75–100mm of firm sod above sand level in bunker which defines the bunker edge nearest green; should be cut vertically.

**Liquid fertiliser**   Applies to nutrients in solution which may be distributed evenly over turf surface.

**Maintenance building**   Permanent fireproof structure which functions as personnel headquarters, for maintenance, protection, storage of equipment and chemicals etc.

**Mat**   Development of ineffective roots and soil particles; usually occurs between turf surface and original soil level; may be associated with turf that is top-dressed regularly with soil.

**Mowing of fine turf**   This operation must always be executed with finesse; a change in mowing direction on each occasion is important.

**Nursery turf**   Constantly maintained area of good quality turf available for immediate renovation of green, tee or fairway.

**Over-seeding**   Reseeding of existing turf, usually associated with maintenance or renovation of turf surface.

**Parts per million (PPM)**   Number of parts by weight or volume of concentrate to one million parts to form prescribed mixture.

**Pegged turf**   Use of wooden skewers left flush with the surface to hold turf in place on slopes etc., to permit firm rooting to occur.

**Perennial**   Plant that flowers year after year retaining life in its roots through the dormant or non-flowering season, e.g. couch grass (*Cynodon dactylon*).

**Pesticide**   Any chemical material used to control insects destructive to cultivated crops.

**Phytotoxicity**   Material which will injure or kill plant life.

**Plugging turf**   Propagation of turf by initially planting small pieces of sod spaced as required. Turf may be repaired by this method also. Suitable tool for cutting pieces would resemble hole-cutter, i.e., larger or smaller model.

**Practice fairway**   Spacious area within reasonable distance of first tee where members may practice with all clubs at any time, and be provided with tees, bunkers and distance markers, and maintained accordingly.

**Practice green**   Smaller green in vicinity of first tee complete with bunkers, where members may chip and putt.

**Practice putting green**   Area of turf situated near club house and maintained to putting green standard; should be large enough to accommodate 18 holes, and surface conformation in accord with other greens on course.

**Pre-emergence herbicide**   Chemical applied to control any plants as they germinate in soil prior to seeding.

**PSI**   Pounds per square inch.

**Rake for greens turf**   Attachment with spring steel tines fitted in front of cutting cylinder of mower to remove grass stems, and grainy growth.

**Reel or cylinder mower**   Machine with driven cutting cylinder composed of specified number of blades.

**Rhizome**   Underground stem which produces roots and shoots at each node, e.g. *Cynodon dactylon* (couch grass).

**Rippling**   Wavy, or corrugated effect resulting from mowing with maladjusted cutting cylinder, or worn cutting cylinder bearings.

**Rotary mower**   Used to cut grass by impact with grass stems, with high-speed blades operating in horizontal plane.

**Scald**   Result of grass being temporarily covered with shallow water which becomes heated above normal temperatures by sun.

**Scalping**   Removal of all grass by mowing at extremely low level; may only be evident on ridges on uneven surface. Raise mowing height to more suitable level.

**Scum**   Usually caused by algae on surface of fine turf; when dry becomes brittle.

**Slicing**   Turf cultivation by mechanically operated vertically rotating flat blades which slice through the turf at controlled depth.

**Sod-cutter**   Machine designed to cut turf to given width, and adjustable thickness; some machines also provide for cutting turf into lengths.

**Soil fumigant**   Material such as methyl bromide that will kill most organisms in soil. Allow short period after application before planting or sowing may be undertaken.

**Soil probe**   Small diameter tube sharpened at end for extracting soil or turf samples.

**Soil sterilent**   Material which will kill all vegetation and prevent re-establishment for some time.

**Species**   Classification next below genus of animals, or plants having certain distinctive characteristics in common.

**Spiking**   Method of turf cultivation by thrusting solid square fork-tines into turf and soil. Similar result can be obtained by using spike roller which has frames of adjustable spikes which move allowing spikes to rise from turf without any disruption to surface.

**Spot-spraying**   Application of weedicide to small areas or to individual weeds. Dilution rate must be adjusted accordingly.

**Surfactant**   Wetting agent added to spraying mixtures to facilitate even coverage of chemical.

**Syringing**   Hand-watering which is often sufficient in certain circumstances.

**Tee box**   Metal frame on four legs placed at each tee with containers for water, sand, and litter. Metal plate usually attached showing distance of hole and par thereon.

**Tee markers**   Consist of movable solid material, often of cement, placed to denote teeing ground; may be several sets in place at any one time, coloured for different standards.

**Teeing ground**   Starting point for all holes as stipulated by markers; two club lengths in depth.

**Texture**   Overall appearance of turf quality; usually includes purity of species, density of grass leaves and cover without grain or thatch or other noticeable species.

**Thatch**   Undesirable, consisting of dead and living stems, usually above and not actually attached to soil.

**Top-dressing**   Special soil mix of fertilisers and maybe other organic material, prepared and allowed to mature preparatory to spreading and working into turf, usually in dry conditions. In certain circumstances mixture may be worked into turf as slurry.

**Turf burn**   May be result of accidental chemical spill during handling, or from broken pipe or hose during application.

**Turf grass quality**   Visual acknowledgement of turf standard for given purpose.

**Turf management**   Turf cultural practices developed and performed for healthy growth of specified turf type for special purpose or sport.

**Undulation**   Any surface deviation such as hollows and rises; when applied to turf must be formed to proportions to permit exactness of mowing techniques to be performed.

**Vegetative planting**   Asexual propagation using selected pieces of turf sod, or growing stems planted into prepared soil.

**Vehicular road**   It is important to provide for course vehicles to move freely through rough with access to all greens; to be obscured by plantations as far as possible.

**Vertical cutting**   Mechanically driven rotating blades which operate on vertical plane and cut into the turf for the control of surface thatch or grain.

**Vertical or flail mowing**   Type of mower often driven by power take-off shaft, operating blades on vertical plane at high speed for impact result.

**Watering in**   Certain applications of fertilisers or chemicals often require washing or diluting into the soil immediately to prevent any undesirable after-effects on turf.